Transferable
Academic
Skills
Kit

TASK

University Foundation Study

Transferable Academic Skills Kit

Teacher's Book

Jane Brooks

UNIVERSITY OF
READING | *Garnet*
EDUCATION

Published by
Garnet Publishing Ltd.
8 Southern Court
South Street
Reading RG1 4QS, UK

ISBN 978 1 78260 252 1

British Library Cataloguing-in-Publication Data
A catalogue record for this book is available from the British Library.

Production
Project manager: Clare Chandler
Editorial team: Jane Brooks, Clare Chandler
Design & layout: Madeleine Maddock

Garnet Publishing and the authors of TASK would like to thank the staff and students of the International Foundation Programme at the University of Reading for their respective roles in the development of these teaching materials.

All website URLs provided in the Student's Books were correct at the time of printing. If any URL does not work, please contact your tutor, who will help you find similar resources.

Printed and bound in Lebanon by International Press: interpress@int-press.com

Contents

Introduction

What is *TASK*?

The *Transferable Academic Skills Kit* (TASK) was written by English lecturers working on the University of Reading International Foundation Programme. It was produced to address problems faced by international students entering English-medium universities for the first time and to meet their needs. Originally produced as an online resource, the material was tested and adapted over several years, before being developed and enhanced for a wider audience, and published in book form. This second edition has been substantially revised and updated to reflect changes in higher education and technology.

The first module explains the key skills and conventions that students need in order to be successful in higher education. The subsequent modules raise awareness of and help develop a range of transferable academic skills. These include conventions and skills involved in researching and writing academic texts, with particular emphasis given to using online sources; organisational skills such as those involved in teamwork and exam preparation; and spoken skills needed for giving presentations and participating in seminars. There are also modules that help to develop numeracy, problem-solving and critical thinking skills, which support students' ability to complete academic tasks successfully.

Who is *TASK* for?

TASK is designed for international students at all levels, particularly those taking pre-sessional or foundation year courses. It is suitable for students studying a broad range of academic disciplines. The clear, step-by-step approach means that it is also suitable for students who have been studying in the British education system, but who need help in developing practical skills, such as handling statistics and using online sources, or who are unfamiliar with higher education conventions, such as how to reference their work. The range of skills addressed is equally applicable to students studying at higher education institutions in Britain or in other countries around the world.

What do the modules comprise?

Each module is typically divided into six units and is laid out clearly and consistently so that there is a logical progression to familiarise students with all aspects of the topic. Images and diagrams are provided to clarify concepts and stimulate ideas. The modules are designed so that, where written answers are required, answers can be written directly onto the Student's Book page. This allows students to collect their thoughts and ideas in one place, and facilitates reflection. However, there is a Notes section at the end of each Student's Book for when longer written answers are required, or more space needed.

Units contain tasks that help students with terminology and vocabulary, raise awareness of how theory relates to practice and provide practice in using key transferable skills. Tasks are carefully designed to build on previous work so that students can tackle more complex tasks as scaffolding is gradually removed.

At the end of each unit, there is a Reflect section that encourages learners to relate and reapply the skills studied in the unit to their own learning context, and transfer new skills to real-life situations.

Each module concludes with suggestions for extension activities and useful websites. There is also a glossary of high-frequency academic terms used in that module. The glossary can be used as an aide-memoire to remind students of the key terms in the book. It can also be used as a mini-dictionary. If the series is used for classwork, students should be encouraged to refer to the glossary when necessary and to select and record the lexis they will need for active use, e.g., categorising words in mind maps and tables. Teachers may use the glossary terms as the basis for additional vocabulary work and activities, e.g., gapfills, matching words and definitions.

How should *TASK* be used?

The *TASK* series is an extremely flexible learning resource. It can either be followed as a complete course, or individual modules can be selected according to students' specific needs. The materials can be used in face-to-face classes, form the basis for a blended delivery, or made available to students as independent study materials.

The activities involve using a range of skills and strategies, both spoken and written, for a variety of academic purposes. The activities include the following: discussing opinions and questions in pairs and groups; reaching a consensus; planning written work and presentations; solving problems and evaluating different approaches; reading, analysing and evaluating texts; and using scholarly sources, e.g., citing, quoting and reformulating the ideas and words of others.

Some modules also include collaborative practice and role play of academic situations, such as giving a presentation, taking specific roles in a teamwork situation and taking part in a seminar.

Each unit builds towards a Reflect section designed to help students consider how they will transfer their newly acquired skills to their future learning context. Students may be unfamiliar with this type of activity and need support in learning how to reflect on their learning in the early stages.

A number of activities are designed to be completed in groups or pairs. The teacher may wish to focus on the oral work in class and set some of the written tasks for homework if time is limited.

If students are working independently outside the classroom environment, they should be encouraged to collaborate with other students for the purpose of such group work activities. This collaboration could take a face-to-face or online form. Where student collaboration is desirable but unfeasible due to the teaching and learning context, the tutor could work through group or pair activities with students during feedback and progress tutorials.

Students who progress confidently through the module can work independently to complete the Web work and Extension activities sections at the end of the module, whereas students who require additional support can work together with peers to complete these sections.

Using the Teacher's Book

The *TASK Teacher's Book* provides answer keys and model solutions for the exercises in each module where appropriate. Suggestions are also made to assist with the logistics of classroom teaching and additional follow-up ideas are provided.

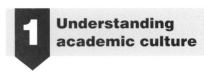

Academic Culture

1 Understanding academic culture

At the end of this unit, students will be able to:

* understand key terminology and concepts relating to academic culture

Task 1 Defining academic culture

Lead in by asking students to focus on the photo and then describe a food-related experience in another country which surprised them. Explain that life in a new academic institution may be full of surprises due to a mismatch between their cultural expectations and the culture of their new place of study.

1.1 Individual work/Pairwork

Students follow instructions in the Student's Book.

Answers:
a. beliefs
b. attitudes
c. culture
d. regulations
e. philosophy
f. research
g. thinking

For a lower-level group, it might be worth giving students two options to choose from for each item, e.g.:
a. beliefs/study
b. attitudes/research
c. thinking/culture
d. regulations/philosophy
e. study/philosophy
f. culture/research
g. thinking/beliefs

1.2 Pairwork

If necessary, give your students a few minutes to write notes in preparation for the speaking activity. You could ask students to record their speaking and use the recording as the basis for a short piece of writing.

Answers:
Answers will vary from student to student.

Task 2 Important words in academic culture

2.1 Classwork

Ask students to identify the three activities shown in the photos. Then ask them whether they have ever participated in a tutorial/seminar/lecture (in English).

Answers:
a. tutorial
b. seminar
c. lecture

2.2 Individual work/Pairwork

Students follow instructions in the Student's Book.

Answers:
a. 6   f. 7
b. 9   g. 8
c. 4   h. 3
d. 2   i. 5
e. 1

2.3 Individual work/Pairwork

Students work individually, and then compare their answers with a partner's.

Answers:
a. lecture   f. further education
b. teaching assistant   g. optional courses
c. plagiarism   h. Humanities
d. personal tutor   i. postgraduate
e. summative assessment

It might be worth pointing out to students that some UK universities use alternative terms, such as teaching assistant (tutorial fellow). It may also be worth adding that tutors can play a more central role in some seminars than the Student's Book definition suggests, depending on the circumstances.

2.4 Pairwork/Small group work

A possible extension activity to revise the vocabulary and the use of defining relative clauses in definitions might be to ask students to write definitions of five or six of the terms of their choice for homework, leaving out the term being defined. These definitions could then be given to another student to complete with the missing term in a later class.

An alternative extension activity to practise the vocabulary would be to ask students to carry out internet-based research to find out about their (future) programme, e.g., On your future programme, what is the balance between:

* **core courses** and **optional courses**?
* **formative assessment** and **summative assessment**?
* **lectures** and **seminars**?

2 The transition to higher education

At the end of this unit, students will be able to:
* identify common challenges for students in the early stages of higher education
* offer useful advice to students

Task 1 Identifying challenges

The purpose of this task is to allow students the freedom to talk about what has been difficult for them personally and to share this with other students who may have had similar problems. It may be that it is the non-academic aspects of the transition from secondary to tertiary education which have caused them the most difficulty.

1.1 Small group work

Encourage students to find more than one challenge for each photo.

Possible answers:
a. adapting to life away from home/cooking
b. organising one's own time/doing research/writing essays or reports/becoming an independent learner
c. sitting exams/attending lectures
d. adapting to life away from home/making new friends/ managing study-life balance

1.2 Individual work

Encourage students to add their own ideas about other challenges.

Answers:
Answers will vary from student to student.

1.3 Pairwork/Classwork

Encourage students to give reasons for their choices.

Answers:
Answers will vary from student to student.

Task 2 Offering advice

2.1 Individual work

Students follow instructions in the Student's Book.

This task offers the opportunity to revise language of similarity, difference and degree. You could provide your students with sentence heads to use for the task, e.g.:
We are fairly alike because …
The main difference between us is …
The two of us are different as …

Answers:
Answers will vary from student to student.

2.2 Pairwork

Students follow instructions in the Student's Book. Alternatively, *Task 2.2* could be set as a piece of writing, with advice for each problem being written on separate pieces of paper. These could form a wall display.

Possible answers:
a. Identify slots in the timetable for self-study and timetable work in. Use a diary to note the deadlines for all assignments. Think about the process of producing the piece of written work. Break the process down into steps, e.g.:
  * analyse the title
  * read around, making notes
  * plan
  * arrange a tutorial to discuss the plan
  * first draft
  * get feedback
  * second draft
  * proofread
  * estimate the amount of time needed for each step, and plan the time backwards from the deadline
b. Use the course reading material to help extend vocabulary. Keep a vocabulary record that includes information on meaning, pronunciation, collocation and grammar of words and phrases.
c. Read module and programme handbooks carefully. Talk to tutors about course requirements and their expectations of your work. Ask other students if they can show you examples of 'successful' work.
d. Prepare carefully for seminars by reading recommended texts and reviewing lecture notes. Show that you are participating in seminars, even if you feel too daunted to speak initially, by using active body language. Try and speak early on in the seminar. Make your tutor aware if you are having problems.

Task 3 Asking for help

Students' concerns may range from practical problems, e.g., opening a bank account and finding suitable accommodation, to more complex ones, e.g., feeling homesick and encountering racism. To set the tone for this task, it might be useful to initiate the discussion by asking students to think about a time in the past when they shared a personal problem with a friend, and to consider how they felt, how the friend reacted, whether the discussion had a successful outcome, and what factors made the outcome successful or otherwise.

3.1 Pairwork

Ask the pairs to identify several common issues. Examples of difficulties might include poor time management or difficulties encountered in a particular module. Encourage students to think about appropriate ways of discussing the issue with a tutor. If helpful, supply students with a list of points to reflect on, e.g.:
* Should you arrange a meeting with your tutor in advance, and if so, how?
* In the meeting, how long should initial pleasantries last?
* To what extent should you express your problem directly?

- How can you signal to your tutor that you are taking the advice in?

It might be worth mentioning the following points, if they don't arise in the discussion.

- It is a good idea to make an appointment with your tutor in advance, e.g., send an email briefly outlining the problem and requesting a meeting. Alternatively, check your tutor's office hours.
- It is important to recognise that the tutor is, in all likelihood, very busy. This means that there may only be a minute or two of pleasantries at the beginning of the meeting, after which the student needs to state the problem and provide any necessary background information.
- The tutor may refer the student on to someone else. This does not necessarily mean the tutor is lazy or uninterested; it may be that the institution employs other specialists to deal with the type of problem the student is experiencing.
- It is a good idea to thank the tutor at the end of the meeting.

3.2 Pairwork

If possible, ask pairs to record their role-play. The pairs can then form small groups and play their recordings to each other within the group. The group can then evaluate the extent to which the role-play followed the criteria for a successful tutorial they established in *Task 3.1*. Individual meetings with staff worry many students. If you think this is the case for your students, you may wish to extend the role-play.

 3 **Expectations of higher education institutions**

At the end of this unit, students will:

- be more aware of the expectations about teaching and learning in higher education institutions

Task 1 General expectations

1.1 Individual work/Group work

Lead in by eliciting what expectations students have about lectures (or assessments/study-life balance). Then ask why these expectations may be disappointed.

Answers:
a. D
b. F – Students should check past exam papers.
c. T – In many UK institutions, the pass mark is 40%, and a mark of 60%–69% is equal to a 2.1 degree in many cases.
d. F
e. F – Extracurricular activities are usually of great importance in student life.
f. D – Students should check programme and module handbooks.

g. D – It is common for students in the UK to leave home in order to attend university.
h. F – This would be unusual.
i. D – Students should check programme and module handbooks.
j. T – Generally speaking, only about the top 10%–20% are likely to achieve a first.

Students should be encouraged to check which of the above are true for their (future) institution of study as there is likely to be some variation.

1.2 Pairwork

Students follow instructions in the Student's Book.

Answers:
Answers will depend on students' expectations.

Task 2 Expectations of lecturers

2.1 Pairwork

Students follow instructions in the Student's Book. Don't provide answers at this point, as these are covered by *Task 2.2*.

2.2 Pairwork

Students follow instructions in the Student's Book.

Answers:
A lecturer would be expected to:
a. give lectures relevant to the subject – if the lectures are uninteresting to the student, maybe he or she is on the wrong course.
b. supply lecture handouts – these are often made available on the web.
e. set and mark assignments, though in many cases a teaching assistant may do the marking.
g. generally, lecturers know and use students' first names, but this can depend on the size of the class.
h. generally, this is true, but it is always a good idea to observe other students' behaviour if you are unsure.

Task 3 Expectations of students

3.1 Pairwork

Encourage students to add their own ideas.

Answers:

students are expected to ...
a. Attend all lectures, seminars and tutorials.
b. Let the lecturer know if they are going to be absent.
c. Take notes from the lecture.
d. Read around the subject of the lecture.
e. Participate in seminar discussions and answer questions.
f. Give presentations.
g. Use the library for research.
h. Participate in group and teamwork activities.

students aren't expected to …
i.   Help the lecturer by cleaning the board or carrying books. j.   Speak to a lecturer if they have a personal problem. k.   Join a university group or club. l.   Get a part-time job to help with finances. m. Buy small presents at the end of the term/semester to thank the lecturer.

Task 4 Critical incidents

Lead in by pointing out that, like much academic English vocabulary, the adjective **critical** can have more than one meaning. Give students some sentences to demonstrate possible differences in meaning, e.g.:

1. My tutor was <u>critical</u> of my argument and suggested I look for better evidence to support my view (i.e., expressing an opinion that something is bad).

2. The peace talks have entered a <u>critical</u> phase (i.e., difficult to handle as a small mistake might result in a much bigger problem).

3. After the car crash, his condition was <u>critical</u> for over a week. After this period, he was moved from intensive care into an ordinary ward (i.e., dangerously ill).

Ask students to read the examples of critical incidents in *Task 4.1* and decide which meaning of **critical** is being used in the term **critical incidents**. (Meaning 2 in the above examples.)

4.1 Pairwork

Students follow instructions in the Student's Book.

Answers:
a.   2.   Apologising at the end of the lecture and giving a suitable excuse.
      1.   This might be appropriate behaviour if a student is late for a seminar that involves a relatively small group of people.
b.   4.   You can still see your parents in the evening.
c.   1.   Serious illness is usually considered mitigating circumstances if a student can provide a doctor's certificate.
d.   3.   Your tutor probably suspects you of collusion. This would be considered a serious incident.

4 Cross-cultural communication

At the end of this unit, students will:
• be more aware of reciprocal speech styles common in English-language academic contexts
• be better able to participate in academic situations, such as seminars

Task 1 Feeling at ease when you speak

1.1 & 1.2 Small group work

Students follow instructions in the Student's Book.

Answer:
1.2
b is the most likely.
Your students may be interested to learn that:
a.   is reserved for medical doctors
c.   is very formal
d.   is very informal

1.3 Classwork

Students may like to discuss the question in pairs before contributing their ideas to a class discussion.

Answers:
Answers will vary from student to student.
Some points to raise, if your students haven't already, might include:
• If you do not know the lecturer at all, use his or her professional title (i.e., not Mr/Mrs/Ms/Miss) and family name, e.g., Dr Meadows.
• If the lecturer asks you to call him/her by his/her first name, it is polite to do so.
• Try to learn lecturers' full names early on in the programme/module. Not using someone's name is considered impolite.

1.4 Pairwork

Students follow instructions in the Student's Book.

Answers:
a.   T
b.   F
c.   T
d.   F – In some cases.
e.   T – Or observe how other students behave.

Task 2 Reciprocal speech style

Lead in by asking students which aspects of seminars are most challenging for them.

2.1 Individual work

Students follow instructions in the Student's Book.

Answers:
1.   b
2.   c
3.   a

In the feedback stage, it might be useful to elicit from students that:

answer = agree or disagree with the question

add = make a claim and provide evidence

ask = either restate the question or ask a closely related question

Task 3 Applying discussion techniques

3.1, 3.2 & 3.3 Pairwork

Explain to students that they should combine one sentence from each of the three tasks to make a discussion point following the ask-answer-add structure.

Answers:

a. Do you think capital punishment is acceptable?

2. (No) All life is sacred.

ii. Would that deter people from committing crimes?

b. Should we ban laboratory testing of cosmetics on animals?

3. (No) There are other ways to do this such as …

v. What do you think about testing new medicines?

c. Should university education be free?

1. (Possibly not) The financial implications would be very heavy.

iv. Who would benefit?

d. Should all students be made to learn at least one foreign language?

4. Communication with different people from different nations is becoming more and more important.

iii. Isn't English a global language?

e. Do you think young people spend too much time online?

5. (I do) More and more young people are suffering from eye strain.

i. What did children used to do in their free time?

3.4 Pairwork

Students should choose one or more of the statements to practise the answer-add-ask structure. If possible, ask students to record their discussions. They can then transcribe these and give the transcriptions to another pair to check for the answer-add-ask steps.

Task 4 Giving yourself time to think

4.1 Individual work/Pairwork

Students follow instructions in the Student's Book.

Possible answers:

techniques	advantages and disadvantages
a. Pretend you haven't heard.	**Advantage:** 'Sorry?' is easy to remember.
	Disadvantage: If you use it too often, everyone might think you are deaf.
b. Repeat the question.	**Advantage:** It sounds natural.
	Disadvantage: You have to remember the question.
c. Use delaying noises.	**Advantage:** These sound natural.
	Disadvantage: You can only use two or three delaying noises, so they buy a little time only.
d. Begin speaking by saying, 'It depends …'	**Advantage:** You don't have to commit to one opinion and you demonstrate that you can see more than one point of view.
	Disadvantage: You can only use this technique if you are being asked for an opinion.

4.2 Individual work/Pairwork

Students follow instructions in the Student's Book.

Answers:

Answers will vary from student to student.

Other suggestions might include:

- Praising the question, e.g., That's a really interesting question.
- Welcoming the question, e.g., I hoped that you might ask me that.
- Promising to think about the question, e.g., I'm really not sure. I would have to think about that one.

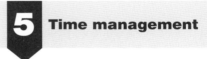

5 Time management

At the end of this unit, students will be able to:

- identify factors involved in good time management
- analyse their own time-management skills and learn how to improve them

Task 1 What is time management?

1.1 Individual work/Pairwork

To lead in, ask students how they would behave in the following situation:

A fellow student has invited you to his/her place for the first time to have a meal at 7 p.m. next Monday.

- What time would you arrive?
- Would you make any preparations? If so, what?
- When would you start making preparations?

Students follow instructions in the Student's Book, and then compare their answers with a partner's.

Answers:

c and e

1.2 Small group work

Ask students to revisit the remaining statements, asking them to alter them to provide more good advice on managing time.

Answers:
Possible changes to the other statements might be:
Time management is …
a. balancing between the quality of the assignments submitted and the time available in which to complete them.
b. managing your time and tasks in such a way as to maximise your learning opportunities.
c. balancing social activities and study in the time before the examination period.
d. organising your time on a day-to-day basis so that you get sufficient sleep.
e. adding your deadlines and appointments to a calendar to help you remember them.

Task 2 Importance of time management

2.1 Individual work

As a lead-in, discuss the diagram with your students, eliciting which are examples of good and bad consequences. Then ask students to add some of their own ideas.

Answers:
In terms of good consequences, possible answers include having time for other activities and not feeling stressed about impending deadlines.

2.2 Pairwork

Ask students to compare their ideas with a partner's, encouraging them to explore the ways in which their ideas are similar and different.

Task 3 Improve your time management

Before students complete this task, it may be useful to discuss the importance of being realistic about their timetables. If the timetable is not based on accurate information, it will quickly become unfeasible.

3.1 & 3.2 Individual work/Pairwork

To encourage students to offer advice and suggestions to each other on their timetables, it might help to give them some sentence beginnings, e.g.:
Have you thought about …
Maybe you could …
One thing which you could think about is …

6 Philosophy of teaching and learning

At the end of this unit, students will be more aware of:
- what constitutes good teaching
- what is involved in learning a subject

Task 1 A good teacher?

As a lead-in, focus students' attention on the visuals and elicit which teacher students think would be a good one and why.

1.1 Pairwork

Ask students to broaden out their discussions to encompass their ideal teacher. Emphasise the need to justify their opinions, eliciting useful language for giving reasons if necessary at the start of the activity.

1.2 Individual work/Pairwork

Ask students to work individually, ranking the characteristics. Then put them into pairs to explain their rankings.

The activity could be extended into a pyramid discussion, with pairs having to decide on their top three characteristics and then pairs of pairs doing the same, and so on until there is a whole-class discussion.

Alternatively, another extension might be to ask students to explain their top three ranking characteristics in writing.

Answers:
Answers will vary from student to student.
(There are no set answers here as students are asked to give their opinions. In the UK, characteristics of a good teacher would probably include a, g, j and ideally i.)

Task 2 The good student

2.1 Classwork

Focus students' attention on the visuals and elicit what activities the various students are engaged in and how these activities are good for study.

Answers:
Answers will vary from student to student.

2.2 Individual work/Pairwork

Like *Task 1.2* in this unit, the activity could be extended to a pyramid discussion.

Answers:
Answers will vary from student to student.
(In the UK, answers b, c, e, f, and j are often considered to be characteristics of good students. As good students progress through their programme of study, however, they will come closer to achieving a, g, and i.)

Module 2 — Group Work & Projects

1 What is *group work* and why is it important?

At the end of this unit, students will be able to:

- identify the key features of group work
- recognise the benefits and challenges of group work
- identify the skills required for effective group work and how it is assessed
- analyse the requirements of a set group project task

Task 1 What is *group work*?

Lead in by asking students to think of the last time they worked in a group to achieve an objective. Ask them to reflect if this was a positive experience.

1.1 Individual work/Pairwork

Ask students to work on the true or false statements individually, and then compare their answers with a partner's.

Answers:
a.   T
b.   T
c.   F – Although this may differ from module to module and institution to institution.
d.   F
e.   T – Occasionally, class time may be allotted to group work.
f.   F – This very much depends on the nature of the project.

1.2 Pairwork/Classwork

Explain to learners that two beliefs prevalent in education in English-speaking countries are that students learn through speaking and that students learn from other students (peers). This accounts, in part, for why group work is a widespread means of assessment. The next activity puts both of these beliefs into practice.

Ask students to discuss with their partner and make a note of their own answers. Pairs of students who finish the task before others in the class can be encouraged to compare and contrast themselves with their partners.

In the feedback stage, ask students to share their experiences with the whole class. If there is time, in a final step, ask students to summarise the class's experience orally or possibly in writing.

Answers:
Answers will vary from student to student.

Task 2 Why group work?

Ask students to read the introduction to the task and elicit what types of challenge they might meet in group work.

2.1 Small group work

Before the lesson begins, allot students to groups and allocate one object per group. Write the expression 'think outside the box' on the board and ask students to guess what it means. Alternatively, show students a brief clip of the TV programme *Dragons' Den*. Having established the goals of the activity, which are to imagine an alternative use for an object and market the idea to an audience, distribute the objects. Students spend 10–15 minutes developing their ideas, making notes as they go.

2.2 Small group work/Classwork

Introduce the presentation task to your students. Depending on the needs of your students, you may wish to elicit useful language for introducing and/or persuading. If you have shown a clip from *Dragons' Den*, you may like to play it again and ask students to make a note of any useful language used by a contestant in their pitch.

Before the presentations are given, explain that the students listening will evaluate each speaker's presentation. Make sure everyone understands that the criterion for success is the *creativity* of the proposal, and not a speaker's language accuracy.

2.3 Small group work

Ask students to discuss the Student's Book questions in their presentation groups. Ask them to take notes of their ideas and to reflect on what they have learned about the benefits and challenges of working in a group through doing the activity.

2.4 Pairwork

Students follow instructions in the Student's Book. Encourage students to justify or explain the reasons behind their choice. If necessary, revise the language for doing this activity.

If there is time, students could be encouraged to share their ideas with the class.

2.5 Individual work

This could be used as a reflection activity, or be set for homework. In either case, students should be helped to understand that goal setting is an important means to maintain motivation and make progress. Ask students to set themselves personal objectives for this module, e.g., I will make at least two contributions in the next class discussion I take part in, and I will use eye contact to encourage others to speak.

Task 3 Assessment of group work

Ask students to read the introduction to the task in the Student's Book and ask your students why their tutors might assess them on the process of group work.

3.1 Individual work/Classwork

Students follow instructions in the Student's Book.

Answers:
a. 5
b. 3
c. 4
d. 1
e. 2

Task 4 Project brief

The endangered species project forms the basis for *Units 2–6*.

Before the lesson, collect a number of pictures of animals, some of which are endangered species. Ask students to name the species and then identify those which are endangered. Ask students to think of examples of endangered species in their country/continent of origin.

If your students use English as an additional language, it may be useful to do some work on the vocabulary and pronunciation of vocabulary related to endangered species at this point.

Ask students to read the project brief carefully. Check their understanding by eliciting, for example:
*   Who will decide the membership of the groups?
*   How many outputs will there be?
*   Which outputs will be assessed through writing? And through speaking?
*   To what extent will you be evaluated on your knowledge of endangered species?
*   To what extent will you be evaluated on your participation in collaborative activities?

Reflect

Encourage students to keep a diary in hard copy or online format in which they collect the various reflection activities which end each unit. Explain that this will help them complete the third stage of the project in which they write a report on the experience of group work.

2 Project planning

At the end of this unit, students will be able to:
*   set goals and objectives
*   plan and organise a group project
*   collaborate to produce a poster

Task 1 Setting goals and objectives

Allocate students to their project groups, and as a lead-in, write *goals* and *objectives* on the board and ask students to discuss the difference between the two terms. At this point, don't explain the difference, but tell students you will ask the same question later in the lesson.

1.1 Small group work

Ask students to discuss questions a–d in their group. Then introduce students to the notion of SMART goals.

1.2 Individual work

Ask students to work individually to identify the three main goals of the project and note these down, and then compare their answers with a partner in their group.

Answers:
*   To produce a poster.
*   To prepare and participate in a debate.
*   To write a reflective report.

1.3 Individual work/Pairwork

Ask students to rewrite their goals as SMART goals, if necessary, and then compare their answers with a partner's.

Possible answers:
*   Our first goal is to design and produce a poster by [date] that features one endangered species.
*   Our second goal is to prepare and participate in a debate on whether endangered species should be protected by researching the topic by [date], coming to a consensus on our group position by [date], preparing for the debate by [date] and conducting the debate on [date].
*   Our third goal is to each write a reflective report on the extent to which our group work experience was successful by [date].

1.4 & 1.5 Pairwork

Ask students to read the introduction to the task and elicit: What is the difference between *goals* and *objectives*?

Give students five minutes to brainstorm in pairs, and then ask them to compare their lists with the one given in *Task 1.5*. They should add any additional tasks they identified in *Task 1.4* to the list, e.g., Make notes on information; keep a careful record of the bibliographic details of each source. Then decide on the best order in which to conduct the steps.

Answers:

1. Choose your topic. Which endangered species will you present on your poster?
2. Check you understand the assessment criteria.
3. Design the poster layout. What will the finished poster look like?
4. Gather information for the poster presentation.
5. Type up each section: description, habitat, etc.
6. Find suitable graphics/images.
7. Prepare a mock-up (first draft) of your poster.
8. Proofread and edit text and graphics.

Task 2 Organising your group project

In order to get your class to think about group roles, you may wish to introduce them to Belbin team role analysis by showing them a relevant graphic; http://www.traininggearasia.com/psychometrics/1936–2/.

2.1 Small group work

Students follow instructions in the Student's Book. If you have introduced Belbin team role analysis, point out its relevance to question d.

2.2 Small group work

As a lead-in, discuss the need to coordinate and organise a project with your students. Ask them what characteristics they would look for in a group coordinator. How would they differ from the characteristics they would look for in a group secretary?

Ask students to discuss and agree on who should take these two roles in their group.

2.3 Small group work

Students follow instructions in the Student's Book.

2.4 Individual work/Small group work

Ask students to work individually to research an assigned online collaborative tool, making notes in the table. This task could be set for homework, with students feeding back to their groups in the following group meeting. Additional online collaborative tools which students could investigate include Mendeley (https://www.mendeley.com/) and Facebook.

Possible answers:
See table below.

online collaborative tool	advantages	disadvantages
Google docs	• free, documents are saved onto Google's servers, so if your computer crashes, you will not lose the document • documents can be shared, opened and edited by many users at the same time • files can be viewed on PCs, tablets and phones	• documents cannot be formatted effectively, so they may lack quality • documents are in the cloud, so are not located in one place • documents cannot be accessed offline • more than one user can work on a document at one time
Skype	• can have group text or audio chats • free communication • it might mean that you feel you do not need to meet with your group members in the flesh	• need internet access • it can be difficult to have a Skype conversation with more than one other person • sound quality may not be good • both users need to be logged in in order to make a free call
Join.me	• useful for video conferences • instant screen sharing • simple interface; easy to use • requires no training • you can record your meetings	• might not work on all computers
vline.com	• you can share your computer screen • easy to set up • can have multi-party video chats • free	

Task 3 Setting deadlines and allocating tasks

Students could either complete the list or create a Gantt chart. For an introduction to Gantt charts: http://en.wikipedia.org/wiki/Gantt_chart or http://www.gantt.com/. For information on how to use Excel to create a Gantt chart: http://www.smartsheet.com/blog/gantt-chart-excel.

3.1 Small group work

Ask students first to think of the stages needed to prepare the poster presentation, then the timing and finally, decide on who will be responsible for delivering each task. Remind them that responsibility for a task may be shared.

Answers:

What needs to be done in order to prepare for the poster presentation?	When should it be done by?	Who is going to do it?
Check you understand the assessment criteria.		
Choose your topic. Which endangered animal will you present on your poster?		
Gather information for the poster presentation.		
Design the poster layout. What will the finished poster look like?		
Type up text for each section: description; habitat, etc.		
Find suitable graphics/images.		
Prepare a mock-up (first draft) of poster.		
Proofread and edit text and graphics.		

Task 4 Producing a poster

4.1 & 4.2 Classwork/Small group work

Students follow instructions in the Student's Book.

Task 4.2 could be organised as a formal poster presentation, which would be particularly appropriate for those students going on to study scientific subjects. Before the posters are displayed, it may be useful to elicit useful language for answering questions to prepare students for a Q&A session.

Reflect

Draw students' attention to the reflection activity and emphasise the importance of keeping their record of reflection up to date.

3 Preparing and presenting ideas in group discussions

At the end of this unit, students will:
- understand expectations for participating in group discussions
- research a discussion topic
- establish their point of view

Task 1 Advice for group discussions

As a lead-in, write *discuss the topic* and *analyse the topic* on the board and elicit the difference between the two instruction words.

1.1 Individual work

Students follow instructions in the Student's Book. This activity may provide an opportunity to introduce your students to useful online resources for learning to take notes: http://learning.londonmet.ac.uk/TLTC/learnhigher/notemaker/.

1.2 Individual work/Pairwork

Ask students to read the statements individually, decide on whether the statements are true, false, probably true, or no information provided, and then compare their answers with a partner's.

Answers:
a. T
b. P
c. ?
d. P
e. ?
f. ?
g. P
h. F

Task 2 Research the topic

2.1 Small group work

Lead in by asking students if they can recall the endangered species introduced by all the different groups in their class.

Students follow instructions in the Student's Book.

2.2 Small group work

Focus students on the activity and elicit the benefits of taking notes in a table – easily able to compare and contrast. If necessary, elicit the characteristics of good notes, selection of key information, use of abbreviations, etc.

Possible answers:

	positive impacts of animal conservation	negative impacts of animal conservation
an endangered species	• animals have the chance to build up their numbers	• extinction of species is a natural part of evolution
the environment	• ecological benefits • biodiversity • maintenance of ecosystem	• over-population of animals may damage the environment
the local people	• economic benefits (tourism, value of land) • aesthetic and recreational activities	• limits development – cannot build houses/factories

2.3 Individual work/Classwork

Write the title and sub-title of the text on the board and ask students to predict:

a. Whether the text will argue that wildlife conservation projects have a positive impact on the environment and on humans.

b. Some of the key vocabulary in the text.

Ask students to skim read to check their predictions.

Then ask students to read and make brief notes. If your students have very different reading abilities, you may like to give weaker readers a smaller section of the text to work on, while stronger readers tackle the whole text.

Students could be asked to give an oral summary of a section of the text, using their notes as a basis for speaking.

Task 3 Using thinking skills

3.1 Pairwork/Classwork

Ask students to discuss points they found surprising in the text. Emphasise that they should explain why they find a point surprising. If your students use English as an additional language, it may be useful to elicit phrases for giving reasons.

Answers:
Answers will vary from student to student.

3.2 Small group work

Students follow instructions in the Student's Book.

Answers:

P ➡ plus points (arguments and ideas *for*)	M ➡ minus points (arguments and ideas *against*)	I ➡ interesting points (arguments and ideas that don't easily fit into the other two columns)
• may lead to jobs in the tourism industry • 'conservation is essential' • ecotourism can create economic and social benefits • ecotourism can increase biodiversity	• the demand for 'pristine beaches' and 'wildlife tours' may lead to developments that do not benefit wildlife • subsistence activities of local communities, such as hunting and collecting wood may be made illegal • 'people-free' areas may be created, which would displace many people • ecotourism does not always lead to sustainable economic development	• people are not always illegal traders, poachers, hunters and habitat destroyers, nor are they always 'wildlife saviours'

Task 4 Doing further research

Students could be encouraged to explore other websites in addition to those given in the Student's Book.

4.1 Individual work

Students follow instructions in the Student's Book.

4.2 Small group work

Students follow instructions in the Student's Book.

The wordle at the end of *Task 4.1* could provide the basis for an activity to recycle key vocabulary. For example, you could use a hot seat activity in which one member of the class chooses a word or expression from the wordle and sits in the hot seat at the front of the class. The rest of the group asks Yes/No questions until one of them correctly identifies the word or expression. That student then goes to sit in the hot seat and the activity continues.

Task 5 Establishing your viewpoint

In order to lead in, you could draw the following diagram on the board and ask students to think where they would place their viewpoint on the diagram.

Endangered species
should not be
protected.

Endangered species
should be
protected.

5.1 & 5.2 Individual work

Students follow instructions in the Student's Book.

5.3 Small group work

When introducing this activity, it is important to emphasise that the aim of the activity is to establish consensus within the time allotted for the activity. At the end of the activity, you may wish to ask how easy or difficult it was for the group to reach agreement, and what factors had an impact on this.

Reflect

Remind students of the importance of maintaining their record of reflection.

4 Communicating effectively in group discussions

At the end of this unit, students will:

- learn useful language for contributing to academic discussions
- practise using these communication strategies
- evaluate their use of communication strategies

Task 1 Useful language for contributing to group discussions

1.1 & 1.2 Individual work/Pairwork

Students follow instructions in the Student's Book.

Complete the first category ('giving your opinion about a topic') as a class (see Answers for suggestions). Students then discuss what they would say in the rest of the situations with a partner before moving on to *Task 1.2* – putting expressions a–v in the correct category.

If your students use English as an additional language, they may need further practice to help them learn the form of the phrases. In this case, students could work in pairs. Write the categories on the board. One student says a phrase and the partner says which category the phrase belongs to. This allows you to monitor and feedback on pronunciation.

Answers:

stating opinions and summarising

1. giving your opinion about a topic
In my experience …
As far as I'm concerned …
Speaking for myself …
In my opinion …
Personally, I think …
I'd say that …
I'd suggest that …
I'd like to point out that …
I believe that …
What I mean is …

2. adding something to what has just been said
a. I'd just like to add …
i. You mentioned X…

3. agreeing with what has been said
c. X put it very well when he/she said …
u. I fully agree with X.

4. disagreeing with what has been said
j. I see what you mean, but …
q. You have a point there, but …
r. I'm afraid I don't agree …
t. It's true that …, but …

5. summarising what has been said
e. On balance, …
i. Overall, …
n. To sum up, …
s. X raised some important points.

asking questions in seminars and group discussions

1. asking a question
m. I have a question about X.
p. I would like to ask you something about X.

2. asking for repetition when you haven't heard what has been said
f. I didn't quite catch that.
o. Could you repeat that, please?

3. asking for clarification when you haven't completely understood the message
d. Could you explain what you meant when you said that …?
h. I'm afraid I didn't follow your point about … Could you go over that again?
k. Could you go over what you said about …?
v. Can I check that I've understood …?

4. interrupting politely
b. If I might interrupt for a moment, …
g. Excuse me, …

Task 2 Communication strategies in context

2.1 Individual work/Pairwork

Students follow instructions in the Student's Book.

Possible answers:
a. Sorry, I didn't quite catch that./Could you repeat that, please?
b. Could you explain what you mean by …?/Sorry, what does X mean?
c. I see what you mean, but …/You have a point there, but … /I'm afraid I don't agree … /It's true that …, but …
d. X put it very well when he/she said …/I'd just like to add …
e. If I might interrupt for a moment, …/Sorry, can I add something here?
f. On balance, …/Overall, …/To sum up, …
g. I'm not sure I completely understand the text. Could you summarise the main ideas?

Task 3 Practise using communication strategies

3.1 Pairwork

Encourage students to give their reasons for agreeing or disagreeing with the statements. Ideally, ask students to record their spoken work in this task to provide a useful basis for *Task 3.2*.

Students can be encouraged to practise using the key language by copying the phrases from *Task 1* onto a set of cards for each pair. These should be equally divided between the pair and then spread out face up in front of their 'owner'. In the discussions, each time a student manages to use one of his/her partner's expressions, he/she takes the card from his/her partner and adds it to his/her cards.

3.2 Individual work/Pairwork

Students should complete the table with language they have used in the discussion activity in *Task 3.1*.

Task 4 Language activation

4.1 Individual work

Students follow instructions in the Student's Book.

4.2 & 4.3 Small group work

Students follow instructions in the Student's Book. Again, it is useful if students can record their spoken work. Reviewing the recordings they have made in the lesson will help them answer the reflection questions.

 Encouraging interaction

At the end of this unit, students will be able to:
• identify verbal and non-verbal clues during conversations
• maintain interactive dialogue in discussion
• identify techniques for encouraging or discouraging interaction

Task 1 Using verbal and non-verbal information

Lead in by eliciting from students how we show agreement when we speak to other people. Hopefully, students will include some non-verbal signals, e.g., nodding the head. Write the suggestions on the board and ask students to categorise the ways of agreeing into verbal and non-verbal ones.

1.1 Individual work/Pairwork

Students follow instructions in the Student's Book.

Answers:
a. 5
b. 1
c. 9
d. 7
e. 2
f. 4
g. 3
h. 8
i. 6

1.2 Larger group work

Students follow instructions in the Student's Book.

1.3 Individual work/Classwork/Larger group work/ Small group work/Plenary

Encourage students to add further strategies and language clues to the list in the Student's Book.

1.4 & 1.5 Individual work/Pairwork

Students follow instructions in the Student's Book.

Answers:
Answers will vary from student to student.

Task 2 Talking at or talking to

Elicit from students what the prefix *inter* means – between people or things. Ask students what the verb *interact* means and ask them to provide an example sentence. Explain that *to talk to* is a synonym for *interact*. Contrast this with the verb *to talk at*.

2.1 & 2.2 Pairwork

Students follow instructions in the Student's Book. Ask students to give reasons for their decisions.

Answers:
2.1
a.   Type B
b.   Type A
c.   Type B
d.   Type A
e.   Type B
2.2
a.   Answers will vary from student to student.
b.   The potential disadvantages of being a Type A person include:
  • a Type B person may dominate the conversation
  • the conversation may go off topic
c.   It may be useful to be a Type B person in situations where keeping control of the dialogue is important, e.g., a school teacher disciplining a pupil.

Task 3 Group behaviour

3.1 Individual work

Students follow instructions in the Student's Book.

Answers:
1.   f
2.   b, c, e
3.   a, d
4.   g

3.2 Small group work

Students follow instructions in the Student's Book.

Task 4 Listening techniques

4.1 Small group work

If you have students in your class who may not know all of the vocabulary in *Task 4.1*, you could mime the appropriate vocabulary.

Answers:
See table below.

4.2 Small group work

Students follow instructions in the Student's Book.

Task 5 Interaction issues

Ask students which discouraging behaviour from the table in *Task 4.1* would bother them most if they encountered it in a discussion.

5.1 Pairwork

Students follow instructions in the Student's Book.

Possible answers:
a.   Find out whether the other person is shy or angry. Maybe there is another reason why he/she did not maintain eye contact.
b.   You could avoid making eye contact with them and say, 'If I could just finish'.
c.   Listen actively by nodding, maintaining eye contact and sitting in an attentive way.
d.   Do not assume the person was bored. There may be another reason for their behaviour.
e.   Thank the person for the question, and then either ask them to answer their own question by saying 'That's an interesting question; what do you think?' or by admitting that you do not know the answer, and that you would find out and get back to the person later.

Answers (Task 4.1):

technique	encourages	discourages	it depends
fidgeting		X	
maintaining eye contact	X		
scowling		X	
smiling	X		
head nodding	X		
looking down		X	
making non-verbal noises, such as *uh-uh* or *mmm*	X		
using exclamations, such as *Really?!*, *Great!* or *Wow!*			X
repeating key speaker words		X	
asking questions	X		
keeping silent			X
folding your arms across your chest and sitting in your chair		X	

5.2 Larger group work

If possible, it is useful to film students working on this activity to provide them with a means of monitoring their behaviour and that of others. Information from the observation can then be used for the subsequent reflection task.

Ask students to select one of the aspects of the unit to discuss, e.g., the variation in non-verbal clues from culture to culture, situations in which being a Type B person might be useful (*Task 2.2*) or inappropriate group behaviour (*Task 3.2*).

Again, remind students of the importance of maintaining their record of reflection.

 6 Evaluating group performance

At the end of this unit, students will be able to:
- apply communication strategies in debates
- evaluate their contributions to a discussion
- evaluate their group's performance
- assess development of their teamwork skills

Task 1 Participate in a debate

Lead in by explaining that the purpose of the debate is to give students further practice of the strategies and language they have used in earlier units. If your students use English as an additional language, it may be useful to revise vocabulary related to the topic of endangered species.

1.1 Classwork/Larger group work

If your class has too many students to run *Task 1.1* as a whole-class activity, divide students into two or more groups, making sure there is a representative mix of students from each of the project groups.

Students follow instructions in the Student's Book.

If your students use English as an additional language, it may be useful to revise the language for indicating a viewpoint and justifying before the debate begins.

Emphasise that each member of the group should contribute, and elicit strategies students can use to encourage others to participate.

If possible, video the debate, or ask students to make personal recordings.

Task 2 What kind of contributor am I?

2.1 Individual work/Pairwork

Students follow instructions in the Student's Book. Encourage students to reflect on their notes and possibly add some SMART goals to their record of reflection.

Ask students to read the conclusion statement at the end of *Task 2.1*. Elicit what tutors may evaluate in a debate – content knowledge and academic skills. Ask students to reflect on how much they have learned about endangered species and their protection during the project.

2.2 Individual work

Ask students to use their record of reflection for this activity. They should look for evidence in their records to support the choices they make in *Task 2.2*.

2.3 Individual work

Write the phrase *to put yourself in someone else's shoes* on the board and tell a story to illustrate its meaning. Ask students to put themselves in the shoes of a tutor and decide which of the points in *Task 2.2* are the most important. Ask students to take notes, justifying their ideas.

Ask students if, when they put themselves in a tutor's shoes, they had a very different view from their own.

Task 3 Evaluating group performance

3.1 Individual work

Again, refer students to their record of reflection. Ask them to use these to complete the table, giving examples to illustrate their evaluations.

3.2 Pairwork

If your students use English as an additional language, it might be useful to revise language of comparison before students move on to the task itself.

3.3, 3.4 & 3.5 Individual work

Draw or show an image of a pair of scales and explain to students that in English-speaking educational cultures, the ability to give a balanced self-evaluation is a highly-prized skill. Then set *Tasks 3.3–3.5*. Encourage students to transfer their ideas to their record of reflection in preparation for preparing the reflective report.

Task 4 Developing your teamwork skills

4.1 Individual work

Ask students to evaluate their confidence in relation to the teamwork skills given in the task.

They could be encouraged to choose two or three of the skills to develop further and express these as SMART goals in their record of reflection.

The statements in the reflection section are designed to be added to the record of reflection. However, they could be debated by the whole class, project groups, or pairs, before being written up.

Extension activities

At this point, you could reintroduce the third project stage – the 500-word reflective report. See Activity 3 on page 36 of the Student's Book.

Ask your students to reflect on Activities 1 and 2. Some students may prefer to record their thoughts in answer to Activity 2, rather than write notes.

Many students find reflective writing challenging, so it may be useful to provide sentence stems that students complete, e.g.:

- It seems to me that …
- In the project group, I tended to play X role.
- I believe that I contributed to X [aspect of group work] well/fairly well/badly because …
- I became frustrated when …
- On balance, I think my experience of working in the group was (un)successful because …
- In hindsight, I wish I had(n't) …
- I wish I had taken more/fewer risks.
- In this project, I think I learned more about X than Y.
- The most useful thing I learned from the group work experience was …
- I wish I had had more time to …
- I wish we had spent less time …
- In future, when I'm working on a group project, I'll never/always …
- The next time I work in a group, I will …

Module 3 Critical Thinking

1 What is critical thinking?

At the end of this unit, students will be able to:
- understand the difference between thinking and critical thinking
- recognise the difference between fact and opinion
- use a framework to evaluate arguments

Task 1 Thinking skills

Explain to the class that the point of the activity is not so much to get the right answer as to examine the process of finding a solution to a problem. Either ask students to work through *Tasks 1.1* and *1.2* individually and then discuss the steps in their thought process with a partner, or ask students to work through *Tasks 1.1* and *1.2* with a partner, verbalising their thought processes as they are doing the task.

1.1 Individual work/Pairwork

Students follow instructions in the Student's Book.

Answers:
a. Carrot   A carrot is not a fruit.
b. Diamond   A diamond is not a metal.
c. Three   It is not an even number.
d. Cooking   Cooking is a hobby that doesn't involve a ball.

1.2 Individual work/Pairwork

Students follow instructions in the Student's Book.

Answers:
a. s
b. 3
c. 21
d. 64
e. n
f. 29

Task 2 Critical thinking skills

2.1 & 2.2 Individual work/Pairwork

After students have read the introduction to *Task 2*, elicit further examples of when they use sequencing or look for patterns in order to achieve a task in their daily lives.

If your students use English as an additional language, you may need to pre-teach the following vocabulary before they read the text:
a global language
to migrate
economic dominance
status

Ask students to read the questions in *Task 2.2* and then read the article in order to answer the questions.

Answers:
a. English has become a global language.
b. Three reasons:
    1. historical – the language migrated with native speakers to many parts of the world.
    2. easy to learn – simple grammar and vocabulary borrowed from many other languages.
    3. economic – economic dominance of some English-speaking countries.
c. English is likely to remain the number one global language for the foreseeable future.
d. The three points do not support the conclusions as none of them adequately explains the future dominance of English.

Task 3 Facts or opinions?

Lead in by focusing students' attention on the picture of the car and the two comments. Elicit which comment is an opinion and which is fact.

Read the introduction to the task and elicit how we would show that the car has a powerful engine. Ask if we could provide evidence of its beauty.

3.1 Pairwork

Ask students to apply the same thinking routine to the statements in this task as they did to the statements about the car, i.e., can it be observed, tested or checked against evidence?

Answers:
English is a very easy language to learn. (opinion)
English is spoken all over the world. (fact)

3.2 Individual work

Answers:
a. English has borrowed many words from a wide range of other languages. Examples include 'tycoon' from Japanese, 'verandah' from Hindi, 'opera' from Italian, 'slim' from Dutch and 'junta' from Spanish.
b. English is spoken in more countries than any other language.
c. English is the language of Shakespeare, so it is superior to other languages.

3.3 Pairwork

Students follow instructions in the Student's Book.

Answers:
Answers will vary from student to student.

Task 4 Questioning opinions

Explain that asking questions of a knowledge claim is a central component of critical thinking. Read the introduction to the task and elicit the three possible positions a thinker can take on a knowledge claim: accept, reject and suspend judgement.

4.1 Small groups

Answers:
a.	Opinion:	Only experts can make decisions on the practice of cloning.
	Questions:	Why can't the general public make decisions on cloning?
	Evaluation:	What is involved in understanding cloning?
b.	Opinion:	Vegetarianism is better than meat eating.
	Questions:	What makes a vegetarian diet better for you?
	Evaluation:	What are the criteria for a 'better diet'?
c.	Opinion:	Economists need to understand history.
	Questions:	How are Economics and history related?
	Evaluation:	Why is knowledge of Economics essential? To what kind(s) of history?
d.	Opinion:	Poor attachment can lead to delinquency.
	Questions:	How is poor attachment linked to delinquency?
	Evaluation:	What do we mean by 'poor'?

Task 5 A checklist for evaluating facts and opinions

5.1 Individual work/Pairwork

Students follow instructions in the Student's Book, and then compare their answers with a partner's.

Answers:
a. unbiased
b. evidence
c. concepts
d. reasoning
e. viewpoints

Task 6 Putting evaluation into practice

Focus students on the photo of Zamenhof and ask if they know his claim to fame. Then elicit what students know about Esperanto.

6.1 Pairwork

Students follow instructions in the Student's Book.

Answer:
The artificial language of Esperanto would be a more appropriate global language than English in the 21st century.

6.2 Pairwork

Students follow instructions in the Student's Book.

Possible answers:
• What is a global language?
• Is Esperanto a global language?
• Is English a global language?
• Will a global language exist in the 21st century?
• What criteria could we use to decide what makes a language appropriate as a global language?

• If Esperanto is an artificial language, what sort of language is English?
• Does the quality of a language (artificial or not) make a language appropriate as a global language?

6.3 Individual work/Pairwork

Remind students of the critical thinking questions they worked on in *Task 5.1*. Ask them to read the essay on page 7 of the Student's Book, applying the questions as they read and taking notes? They should then compare their answers with a partner's.

If your students use English as an additional language, you may need to pre-teach some of the following language:
To bring about
To base X on Y
To sign a petition in favour of X
To reject X
X is evidence of Y

Answers:
Answers will vary from student to student.

2 Recognising strong or sound arguments

At the end of this unit, students will be able to:
• identify parts of arguments
• understand the relationship between the parts of an argument

Task 1 Constructing an argument

Ask students to read the introduction to the unit and *Task 1.1*. Ask them whether, in their experience, the premises always precede the conclusion in a text.

1.1 Individual work/Pairwork

Students follow instructions in the Student's Book, and then compare their answers with a partner's. When feeding back, draw students' attention to the possible positions of a conclusion relative to the premises: before and after.

Answers:
Global warming is definitely happening. I don't care what people say, but it was hotter this year than it has ever been.

1.2 & 1.3 Individual work/Pairwork

Students follow instructions in the Student's Book, then compare answers with their partner's.

Answers:
1.2
a. Ali does not have a visa.
b. Natalia will be travelling by Western Region trains.
1.3
a. Sarah Rollings will win the student election.
b. My cousin will suffer a loss in his profits.

Task 2 Recognising arguments

2.1 Individual work/Pairwork

Students follow instructions in the Student's Book, and then compare their answers with a partner's.

Answers:
a. <u>Some manufactured products contain nuts.</u> Harry is severely allergic to nuts. <u>Therefore he should avoid certain manufactured foods.</u>
b. <u>My aunt has sent me a cheque every year since I was five years old. Therefore I expect to receive a cheque for my birthday this year, too.</u>
c. <u>All Chinese people are good cooks.</u> Li Juan is Chinese so, <u>as a consequence, she must be a good cook.</u>

2.2 Individual work/Pairwork

Students follow instructions in the Student's Book, comparing answers with their partner's.

Answers:
a. 1 The premise about all Chinese people being good cooks is flawed.
b. 2 If Harry eats manufactured food containing nuts, he will absolutely have an allergic reaction.
c. 3 Based on past evidence, my aunt is likely to send me a cheque, but there is a chance she may not.

Task 3 Checking your understanding

3.1 & 3.2 Individual work/Pairwork

Students follow instructions in the Student's Book, and then compare their answers with a partner's. If they are having difficulties, refer them back to the definitions of valid, sound and strong arguments on page 9 of the Student's Book.

Answers:
3.1
a. 1
b. 3
c. 2
3.2
a. F – They can be completely wrong.
b. T – Because the premise is true.
c. F – The premise may not be 100% watertight.

3.3 Individual work/Pairwork

Set a context for this activity by asking students to put themselves in the shoes of a manager. A vacancy has arisen in the manager's department and his/her dilemma is whether to advertise the post outside the manager's company, or whether to advertise it inside the company.

Answers:
a. valid
b. sound
c. strong
d. strong
e. sound

Task 4 Your examples

4.1 & 4.2 Individual work

These two tasks could be set for homework. Students can be encouraged to take examples from their reading and provide a bibliographical reference.

Answers:
Answers will vary from student to student.

4.3 Pairwork/Small group work

An alternative method to the one given in the Student's Book is for pairs to choose and show one strong and one sound argument, not indicating which is which. These arguments could then be displayed on the walls of a classroom, or could be posted to a VLE discussion forum so that the whole class can work on identifying strong and sound arguments.

Reflect

The reflection task could be set as an independent study activity, but could also form the basis of a classroom debate, or a thread on a VLE discussion forum.

 Recognising poor arguments

At the end of this unit, students will be able to:
• recognise weak arguments
• point out weak arguments politely

Task 1 Spotting fallacies in arguments

Show students an example sentence containing the term **fallacy**, e.g.:
In her discussion of corporate social responsibility (CSR), Tavakoli (2013) exposes the **fallacy** that a company which has a CSR policy is necessarily a socially responsible, organisation.

Ask students to read the definition of **fallacy** given on page 12 of the Student's Book and discuss the fallacy referred to in the example sentence.

1.1 Individual work/Pairwork

Students follow instructions in the Student's Book, and then compare their answers with a partner's.

Answers:
a. <u>He hasn't replied, so he can't have received my letter.</u>
b. <u>He does not wear glasses, so he must have excellent eyesight.</u>
c. <u>English is superior to other languages</u> and, <u>as a result, is a global language.</u>
d. <u>I've double-checked my essay, so there can't be any mistakes in it.</u>

Task 2 Poor argumentation strategies

Ask students to read though the four types of poor argumentation strategies.

2.1 Individual work/Pairwork

Students follow instructions in the Student's Book, and then compare their answers with a partner's.

Answers:
a.   3
b.   4
c.   1
d.   2

2.2 Individual work/Pairwork

Students follow instructions in the Student's Book, and then compare their answers with a partner's.

Possible answers:
a.   4   *Our taxes are so high* … This is a complete waste *of taxpayers' money.*
b.   2   *Everyone knows that* …
c.   1   … it is definitely not true *in my case.*
d.   3   Harry Potter novels are *childish* and *unsuitable for adults*, so you should not read them. (Addressed to an adult reader.)

2.3 Individual work/Pairwork

Students follow instructions in the Student's Book, and then compare their answers with partner's.

Possible answers:
a.   The government spent £5 million on multicultural centres that have not been used. This is a waste of taxpayers' money.
b.   Rural life is preferable to urban life because research has shown that rural dwellers have fewer heart attacks than those who live in the city.
c.   Eating five pieces of fruit or vegetables a day has had a significant impact on health according to the *Journal of Nutritional Science.*
d.   Harry Potter novels were written for children, so may not be sufficiently sophisticated for an adult audience.

Task 3 Checking your understanding

3.1 Individual work/Pairwork

Students follow instructions in the Student's Book, and then compare their answers with a partner's. If your students use English as an additional language, you may need to teach the idiom: X makes my blood boil.

Answers:
a.   3
b.   1
c.   4
d.   2

3.2 Individual work

You may need to elicit further examples of softening language before students attempt the activity. Alternatively, ask students to complete the task and then collect examples of softening language on the board.

Possible answers:
a.   Don't you think that is a little conformist?
b.   Aren't you being rather subjective?
c.   Aren't you being rather provocative?
d.   Don't you think you are slightly over-generalising?

 4 Persuasion through language or pressure

At the end of this unit, students will be able to:
- recognise when language, rather than reason, is used to persuade
- recognise when pressure, rather than reason, is used to persuade

Task 1 Making an idea sound better or worse

Ask students to read the introduction to this task and then elicit further examples of contrasting pairs of vocabulary, e.g., She is pig-headed/determined.

1.1 Pairwork

Students work with a partner to complete the task.

Answers:

positive connotations	negative connotations
economical thrifty frugal	stingy penny-pinching mean tight-fisted

1.2 Classwork

If students have their own dictionaries with them, ask them to find out how their dictionary signals that an expression has a positive or negative connotation.

1.3 Pairwork

While students work in pairs, they may like to compare the dictionary entries for each expression found if they have different dictionaries from each other.

Possible answers:
a.   +:   bright, sharp
      -:   nerdy, geeky
b.   +:   expansive, talkative
      -:   garrulous, verbose
c.   +:   under-achieved, missed the mark
      -:   flunked, flopped

Task 2 Making something sound less important or serious

2.1 & 2.2 Pairwork

Students work with a partner to complete the tasks.

Answers:
a. He is just a teacher. = Teaching is a relatively unimportant/ low status career.
b. It costs a mere £20 a month to insure your life. = The outlay of £20 is relatively small for the size of the gain.
c. She got her 'degree' from a university in the Midlands. OR She got her degree from a 'university' in the Midlands. = Her qualification/institution is below standard/low status.

Task 3 Making something seem more important or serious

You may need to teach your students the pronunciation of **hyperbole** /haɪˈpɜːbəliː/.

3.1 Small group work

Depending on the needs of your group, you may need to pre-teach language of speculation.

Possible answers:
a. A cold is not a serious illness. Possibly the speaker has used the hyperbole to cover up the fact that he/she has another reason for not wanting to go to work.
b. The speaker wants the listener to think his/her parents are extremely strict, although asking someone to be home by midnight is not wholly unreasonable.
c. The speaker wants you to think the film is boring and assumes you will be led to believe this by the use of hyperbole.

3.2 Small group work

Students find their own examples of hyperbole and share them with their partners, who speculate on why they might have used the hyperbole.

Task 4 Pressuring the audience

4.1 Small group work

Students follow instructions in the Student's Book.

Answers:
a. 2 – anyone with half a brain
b. 2 – an educated person
c. 1 – it is universally acknowledged
d. 1 – anyone
e. 2 – all intelligent people

Task 5 Using unreliable statistics

Ask students to read the introduction to the task and elicit further examples of potentially misleading statistics.

5.1 Small group work

Students follow instructions in the Student's Book.

Answers:
a. 1. How many dentists were asked?
    2. Did they recommend any other toothpastes?
    3. Were they offered an incentive?
b. 1. How many Americans are eligible to hold a passport?
    2. What do Americans need a passport for?
    3. What number does this represent?
c. 1. What role does this 10% of the brain play?
    2. Are we able to use the other 90% of our brains?

Task 6 Checking your understanding

6.1 & 6.2 Individual work/Pairwork

Students follow instructions in the Student's Book.

Answers:
A: Anyone with half a brain can see that Esperanto is an easier language to learn than English. It doesn't have any irregular verbs … and it has the smallest vocabulary ever of any language.
B: But the 'language' of Esperanto is totally unknown. Who speaks it? No one.
A: Unknown? It has slightly fewer speakers than English, but the difference in numbers is minimal.
B: You're joking! Esperanto only has a handful of speakers and there's a reason for that. It's OK for chit-chat, but you can't have a serious conversation in it.
A: Well, we're speaking English now and I wouldn't call this a serious conversation.

Reflect

Encourage students to provide examples to support their position. If appropriate, ask students to share their essays on a VLE discussion forum and encourage them to assess whether these arguments are valid, sound or strong.

5 **Detecting bias**

At the end of this unit, students will be able to:
- consider sources of bias in evidence in academic research
- identify possible reasons for researcher bias

Task 1 Detecting possible bias – interviews

To set the context for *Task 1.1*, ask students if they have ever been interviewed as part of someone's research. Alternatively, show a few minutes from a YouTube clip of an interview: https://www.youtube.com/watch?v=U4UKwd0KExc.

1.1 Small group work

Students follow instructions in the Student's Book.

Possible answers:
a. They might feel embarrassed to tell the truth. They might want to make a good impression. A *Yes/No* question format might not allow the interviewee to give an accurate answer.
b. The interviewee may shape his/her answers in response to the interviewer's identity.
c. The interviewer can explain his/her background, and reason for conducting the research. He/She can avoid asking leading questions, and not judge or comment on the interviewee's responses.

If you showed an excerpt from the YouTube clip, you may now like to show the complete clip. It contains ten errors on the part of the interviewer, which you can ask your students to find. To correct this activity, play a second YouTube clip, with the interviewer not making the ten mistakes: https://www.youtube.com/watch?v=eNMTJTnrTQQ.

Task 2 Detecting possible bias – Researchers and sources of funding

2.1 Small group work

Students follow instructions in the Student's Book.

Possible answers:
a. The researcher might feel pressure to find positive outcomes for his/her sponsor.
b. The library staff may be tempted to overreport library use in an attempt to justify the library remaining open.
c. The British researcher may be biased against or for the group of migrants.
d. The researcher may feel pressure to find a positive impact of fibre on a diet.
e. The course director may emphasise positive outcomes and minimise negative ones in order to give evidence that he/she is doing his/her job well.

2.2 Pairwork

Students follow instructions in the Student's Book. As a follow-up, students could be encouraged to share with the class examples from their disciplines of researcher bias.

Answers:
Answers will vary from student to student.

Task 3 Avoiding bias

Ask students to read the introduction to the task and elicit if they think that reflexivity is a feature of their future discipline.

3.1, 3.2 & 3.3 Individual work/Pairwork

Students follow instructions in the Student's Book. As students complete *Task 3.1*, they should be able to justify why any of the items they have included in their list of personal information to disclose might be a potential source of bias. As an extension to *Task 3.3*, ask students to find examples of reflexive statements in published research, if relevant to their future disciplines.

Answers:
3.1
Your age
Your religion
Your nationality
Your gender
Your sponsorship
Your profession
Your educational background

Reflect

The reflection task can be extended by asking students to reflect on the place of objectivity in their field of study.

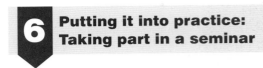

6 Putting it into practice: Taking part in a seminar

At the end of this unit, students will be able to:
- use their critical thinking skills to construct their own arguments
- evaluate their own and others' arguments using their critical thinking skills
- recognise different styles of arguing
- put together the skills they have developed in earlier parts of the module

Task 1 Understanding the question

You may wish to ask students to find some initial sources relevant to this question before the lesson.

1.1 Small group work

If students have brought relevant sources to class, they should draw material from them during this task.

Answers:
a. Students are likely to find a range of definitions of *culture*. Many of these definitions refer to ideas, beliefs and values shared by a group of people.
b. Cultural homogenisation.
c. *Local cultures* share the characteristic of being cultures within cultures.
d. To keep in a certain condition.
e. *Preserve* suggests that cultures can change, but that this process of change can be stopped.
f. Is it possible?

Task 2 Your view

2.1 Individual work

If necessary, model the activity for your class by extemporising your thoughts as you decide where to place your cross on the first continuum. Alternatively, invite a student to do this.

Answers:
Answers will vary from student to student.

2.2 Pairwork

Depending on the needs of your students, you may need to elicit phrases for comparing and justifying. Alternatively, you could provide some sentence heads for students to complete, e.g.:
I think that X because …
The (main) reason I believe that X is …
I think that X for two main reasons.
Our positions are alike in that we both …
Neither you nor I think that …
The biggest difference between us is that you …, while I …

2.3 Small group work

Students follow instructions in the Student's Book. Encourage them to take notes. A possible extension task would be to ask the group to produce a mind map of their discussions.

Task 3 Gathering information

3.1 Small group work

If you predict that your students might get stuck for ideas, on the board, write: *How? Who? Where?* Elicit further question words and phrases from students and add them to the board. Instruct students to use these words as a starting point for brainstorming reading questions.

If you think that question grammar may pose a problem, another lead-in option would be to ask students to unjumble questions, e.g.:
be / ? / can / how / globalisation / defined
globalisation / ? / be / conceptualised / can / how
involve / cultural / ? / what / globalisation / does
most affected / ? / who / globalisation / is / by / cultural

Alternatively, set this task for homework before the class.

Depending on the needs of your class, after the groups have brainstormed questions, you may wish to use their questions as material to recycle question grammar.

Possible answers:
- How can globalisation be defined?
- What are examples of local cultures across the world?
- How would you preserve local cultures?
- Is it possible to preserve local cultures?
- What does cultural globalisation involve?
- Is it important to preserve local cultures?
- What is wrong with cultural globalisation?
- How does cultural globalisation occur?

3.2 & 3.3 Small group work

Depending on the needs of your students, you may need to pre-teach some of the following vocabulary:
portmanteau
infusion
benignly
forlorn
proliferation
to impose a quota
to resort to X
cultural protectionism
to enshrine X
a naysayer

Students follow instructions in the Student's Book. Encourage students to take notes and to include bibliographical details. For more information, see *TASK Module 6: Research & Online Sources*, and *Module 7: Referencing & Avoiding Plagiarism*.

Task 4 Developing your argument(s)

Lead in by asking students to read the introductory text and elicit the relationship between a general argument, more specific arguments, and counter-arguments.

4.1 & 4.2 Individual work

Model *Tasks 4.1* and *4.2* for the class, and then elicit some further examples of arguments and counter-arguments. Where possible, encourage students to use arguments, reasons and examples they have found in the literature. After students have worked on *Task 4.1* for five minutes, encourage them to start thinking of refutations of the counter-arguments.

4.3 Pairwork/Small group work

This activity works well in both pairs and threes. In the first case, students follow instructions in the Student's Book. It is useful if students can record themselves speaking and then review their work. In the second case, the third student comments on the logic of the arguments given by the other two students, then students switch roles. Whichever method is adopted, remind students of the importance of taking notes, as these will be useful for *Task 5*.

If students need reminding of the language for softening feedback, refer them to *Unit 3*, *Task 3.2* on page 14 of the Student's Book. Alternatively, write up some examples of indirect feedback language and ask students what the sentences actually mean. This is a particularly useful activity for students who use English as an additional language as the indirect forms can be confusing for students from more direct cultures. Examples of indirect statements:

'I like the point you made about preserving traditional cultures, but perhaps it was a little overstated.' (*Your evidence is insufficient for the strength of your opinion*.)

'Your conclusion came as something of a surprise.' (*You didn't fully develop an argument*; or *Your premises do not support your conclusion*.)

As an extension activity, ask students to select the most and least persuasive argument they used and write a brief analysis of why each argument was(n't) persuasive.

Task 5 The seminar

If possible, record the seminar so that students can review their own performance and that of the other participants. The teacher can annotate a video of the seminar using videoANT: http://ant.umn.edu/.

If there are no means of recording the seminar available, the daisy-seminar method described below allows written records of the arguments put forward to be made.

5.1 Classwork/Larger group work

If you have a very large class, or a mixture of quiet and talkative students, you might want to consider a daisy-seminar: sit half the class in an inward-facing circle; the other half of the class chooses an already-seated partner and sits behind him/her, facing outward. The inner-circle students participate in the debate, while the outer-circle students remain silent and make notes on their partners' arguments. When the first group of students has completed the seminar, students swap roles and places, and the activity is repeated.

Reflect

Students follow instructions in the Student's Book. You could choose for students to write up any of the three tasks on a VLE discussion forum. Alternatively, students could use videoANT to annotate the video of the debate with their comments.

Module 4 Essay Writing

1 Getting organised

At the end of this unit, students will be able to:
- understand the requirements of writing an academic essay
- analyse essay questions
- organise ideas to produce a clear outline

Task 1 What is an academic essay?

Lead in by asking students to discuss, in pairs, their best and worst essay-writing experiences. After a brief round-up, elicit different types of essay and write students' suggestions on the board. Then ask students to compare the ideas on the board with the list in *Task 1*.

1.1 Small group work

Ask students to underline the words in the essay titles that helped them identify the essay type as they work through the task.

Answers:
a. argument
b. comparison
c. descriptive
d. problem–solution
e. cause and effect

1.2 Small group work

Students follow instructions in the Student's Book.

Answers:
a. introduction
b. body
c. conclusion

1.3 Pairwork/Small group work

In order to prepare the way for the task, you could copy a short 'model' essay onto a card (one per pair/small group), cut it up into paragraphs, and ask students to re-form the essay. They could then use the essay as an example on which to base their discussions in *Task 1.3*. Encourage students to make notes on their discussions, as they can use these in a class discussion at the end of the activity in which they feed back to the class.

1.4 Individual work/Pairwork

According to the needs of your students, you may need to pre-teach the following: to draft (a piece of writing), to edit (a piece of writing), essay outline, paraphrase, proofread (a piece of writing), source material.

Ask students to complete the task, and then compare their answers with a partner's.

Task 2 Analysing the essay question

2.1 Pairwork

This activity could be tackled in a number of ways according to the needs of your students. You could ask pairs of students to explain the differences in meanings between the instruction verbs. Or you could photocopy the table on page 40, cut it up with the verbs and the definitions separated, and then ask students to match the verbs with their definition.

Alternatively, you could photocopy the table on page 40, cut up each instruction verb and its definition and use these in a vocabulary snowball activity. For this, give each student a word and ask him/her to read it, check any unknown vocabulary in a dictionary, and then learn the instruction verb and its meaning. Students should then move around the classroom, teaching their word to a classmate, who reciprocates. When both students have finished explaining their word, the pair swaps words. Each students then looks for a new classmate to teach his/her new instruction verb and definition to, swapping words again, and so on until the whole group has learned all of the words. At the end of the activity, ask students to complete *Task 2.1* on page 4 of the Student's Book.

2.2, 2.3 & 2.4 Individual work

Students follow instructions in the Student's Book.

Answers:
2.2
Key ideas: problems, traffic congestion, solutions.
2.3
It is a problem–solution essay.
Instruction words: discuss, suggest, evaluate.
2.4
Who is affected by traffic congestion?/What issues arise from traffic congestion?

2.5, 2.6 & 2.7 Pairwork/Small group work

Students follow instructions in the Student's Book.

Answers:
Answers will vary from group to group.

Task 3 Brainstorming ideas

Explain to students that once they have understood the essay task, the next stage is to brainstorm ideas on the topic of the essay.

3.1 Individual work/Classwork/Small group work

Model free writing for your students on the board, explaining that they should keep their pens/pencils on the paper at all times, and that they should aim to write continuously for two minutes. Tell them that this is possible as they are not expected to edit their ideas, but simply write whatever comes into their heads on the topic of transporting goods by road. When they have done this, put them to work in small groups, comparing their texts for similar ideas, or themes. Have a whole-class debrief in which you collect ideas on the board.

3.2 Small group work

Lead in by asking your students to close their eyes and picture a lorry in the middle of a town. Elicit whether the image they saw was a positive one, e.g., a lorry delivering medicines to a hospital; a neutral one; or a negative one, e.g., a lorry stuck in a traffic jam with black fumes coming out of the exhaust.

Introduce the topic of banning lorries from town- and city-centres, asking students to contribute any ideas that come to mind on the topic. Students brainstorm individually before sharing their ideas in groups.

If you would like groups to share their work with the class, for the group-brainstorming step, provide a large sheet of paper and pens, or a computer and projector.

Before you move on to the next task, you could elicit from students which method they preferred: brainstorming individually through free writing, or bouncing ideas off each other in a group.

Task 4 Organising your ideas

Before setting *Task 4.1*, ask students to work in small groups analysing the question. Refer students back to *Unit 1, Task 2*.

4.1 Individual work

Set this activity as individual work, explaining that after five minutes the small groups will re-form to exchange ideas.

4.2 Small group work

This activity usually goes well if you provide students with large sheets of paper/board space and some post-it notes. This allows students to move ideas around, before fixing them in place and connecting ideas with arrows. Allow 15–20 minutes for this stage. Each group should then present their poster in a whole-class activity.

Possible questions your students might address include:
*   Who suffers from traffic congestion?
*   What problems arise because of traffic pollution?
*   What are possible solutions?
*   Which are the best solutions? Why?
*   Which solutions are not effective? Why?

If you feel peer evaluation would be useful at this juncture, elicit criteria for feedback on the mind maps from the class and write these criteria on the board. Assign each group the task of working together to evaluate another group's mind maps. Ask each group to choose one member to act as a scribe, who writes the group's comments on a post-it note and then sticks it onto the relevant part of each mind map.

Posters could then form a wall display. Alternatively, students could take photos of their posters and upload them to an online wall, e.g., Padlet.

2 Getting started

At the end of this unit, students will be able to:
*   start writing an essay
*   write a thesis statement
*   write an effective introduction

Task 1 What to include

The purpose of this task is to encourage students to select relevant information and to prioritise the selected information before organising it in a logical way.

1.1 Individual work/Pairwork

First, ask students to evaluate the importance of the points individually and then ask them to discuss their ideas in small groups. There may be some variation in answers, depending on the line of argument students wish to pursue.

Answers:
a. I
b. U   – This could be background information, but should not make up a major part of the essay.
c. NI
d. I   – The students should be encouraged to see that what is required is not so much a list as an evaluation of these solutions.
e. U/NI – Students should be encouraged to carry out research to find supporting evidence. They should probably broaden the scope of the essay beyond their immediate surroundings.
f. I   – Arguments for or against the various solutions should form the main body of the essay.

1.2 Individual work

First, ask students to evaluate the importance of the points individually and then ask them to discuss their ideas in small groups. There may be some variation in answers, depending on the line of argument students wish to pursue.

Answers:
Answers will vary from student to student.

Task 2 Information gathering

2.1 Pairwork

Encourage the pairs to think of types of information source.

Possible answers (depending on availability):
a. books
b. journal articles
c. websites
d. documentaries

2.2 Individual work/Classwork

This task offers the opportunity for students to evaluate their strengths and weaknesses. The discussion provides you with an opportunity to find out which skills areas worry your students most, and this information could provide a rationale for some remedial work on areas of perceived weakness.

Answers:
Answers will vary from student to student.

Task 3 Arousing interest: The introduction

As a lead-in to *Task 3* you could photocopy a number of introductions to essays on topics with which your students are familiar and ask them to choose a preferred introduction, giving reasons for their choice.

3.1 Individual work/Pairwork

Students follow instructions in the Student's Book.

Answer:
1

3.2 Individual work/Pairwork/Classwork

While students are writing, circulate and correct any language errors in their work. At the end of the task, collect some examples of introductory sentences for one of the essay topics on the board. Then ask students to work in pairs, discussing which sentence they prefer and why. Elicit preferences and reasons in a brief whole-class activity.

Answers:
Answers will vary from student to student.

Task 4 Writing a thesis statement

4.1 Individual work

If your students are unfamiliar with the notion of a controlling idea, you should model the first example on the board.

Answers:
a. HOW the criminal justice system functions in my country.
b. The QUESTIONS left unanswered by the Big Bang Theory.
c. TWO SOLUTIONS to coping with sea-level rises:
   • education on the effects of sea-level rises
   • accurate forecasting of its hazards

4.2 Individual work

Draw students' attention to the language issues related to the essay organisation signposting section:
a. Use of impersonal subject, e.g., This essay starts by discussing definitions of … (NOT 'I will start …').
b. Choice between will/present simple, e.g., This essay will first outline … and then it will discuss … or This essay first outlines … and then it discusses …
c. Typical sentence structures, e.g., In the first section, X is defined. (prepositional phrase + passive voice) or The essay first defines X. ('The essay' as subject + active voice.)

Ask students to use a variety of structures to complete *Task 4.2*.

4.3 Individual work

Model this task for your students, possibly taking two different views about possible solutions to the problems of traffic congestion and showing how the different views would result in different thesis statements. Circulate and correct your students' work where necessary.

4.4 Individual work

Return to the two examples you modelled in *Task 4.3* and show your students how the signposting statements would differ due to differences in the thesis statements. Circulate and correct your students' work where necessary.

Possible answer:
There is growing agreement that the way to control the congestion that ruins our towns and cities is to tax the motorist. This essay will argue for the use of various taxation policies to address the traffic congestion problem in Britain, using Manchester and Edinburgh as examples. It will first evaluate congestion charging as one possible solution, and then discuss the effect of motorway tolls.

Task 5 An effective introduction

5.1 Classwork/Small group work

You could photocopy the sentences of the introduction onto card, one copy per small group, and ask students to work in their groups to re-form the introduction.

Alternatively, you could turn this activity into a running dictation by cutting up one copy of the sentences and blu-tacking the sentences onto one wall of your classroom. Ask students to work in pairs, one playing the role of runner and the other that of scribe. Create a line of desks at one end of the classroom, opposite the wall with the sentences on it. Ask the scribes to sit at these desks. Clear the other furniture to the side of the room to provide a clear path for the runners. Give each scribe five strips of paper to write the five sentences on. Tell the runners to run to the other end of the room, read a sentence and memorise as much of it as possible, including the punctuation, and then run back to their partner and dictate. The scribe notes down the dictation. The runner returns to memorise the next part, and so on. When all the sentences have been written down by the scribe, the pair should organise the five sentences into a general–specific introduction. The pairs who finish quickest can then compare the accuracy of their dictation with the sentences given in the Student's Book.

Answers:
a. 3
b. 2
c. 5
d. 4
e. 1

5.2 Pairwork

Students follow instructions in the Student's Book.

Answers:

a. Statements a, b and e are general statements. They give important background information to help the reader understand the context of the problem.

b. Statement c is the thesis statement. The essay will follow the order outlined in the thesis statement and will focus on evaluating solutions (the controlling idea).

c. The body of the essay will require at least six paragraphs as sentence d lists four direct problems and two knock-on problems. The essay will probably be organised as a problem–solution–evaluation essay.

5.3 & 5.4 Individual work/Pairwork

Ask students to apply the criteria in *Task 5.3* to the introduction given in *Task 5.4* and make notes in their Student's Book.

Answers:

Answers will vary from student to student. However, your students should notice that the thesis statement fails to explain the focus of the essay, though it can be inferred that the essay will examine the effects of GM foods on the environment and human health.

5.5 Individual work/Pairwork

Take in and correct the introductions. Ask students to prepare a corrected copy of their introductions for a peer evaluation session in the next class. Encourage students to refer back to the criteria listed in *Task 5.3* to help with the task of evaluating the introductions.

 3 The body of the essay

At the end of this unit, students will be able to:
* structure the main part of an academic essay
* plan and write effective paragraphs

Task 1 Paragraph organisation

1.1 Individual work/Classwork

Students follow instructions in the Student's Book.

Answers:

a. T

b. T/F – Answers to this statement may vary. An analysis of published research indicates that not all professional academic writers use a topic sentence at the start of every paragraph. However, many teachers like to treat the statement as true, particularly with lower-level groups.

c. T

d. F – Examples, figures and statistics are three types of supporting material. There are other types too, depending on the discipline, e.g., paraphrasing/ quoting opinions given in authoritative sources.

e. F – As noted above, support can be given through quoting other authorities, but you can also paraphrase.

f. T

1.2 Individual work

Students follow instructions in the Student's Book.

Answers:

1. The first episode in the Coca-Cola story is an important part of the rise of capitalism in the United States of America. Towards the end of the 19th century, America gradually began to transform itself from a nation of farmers to a city-based, industrialised society. The industrial revolution was epitomised by new communications and the arrival and spread of the railways. This produced a new kind of capitalism, a distinctive American variety, where the ethos centred firmly on the image of individual immigrant struggle. The world of US business was on its way.

2. One of the most important changes, which helped business success, was population growth. The American population almost doubled in size between 1880 and 1910, and a large proportion of the increase was created by the new immigrants from Europe and the rest of the world. Success came from ambition and hard work, and anybody could make large amounts of money provided they tried hard enough. Helped by the success of some, immigrants flocked to the USA. By 1890, there were already over 4,000 American millionaires and Andrew Carnegie, who had made a fortune from railways and iron and steel, was spreading the 'Gospel of Wealth'.

3. There were, however, some disadvantages to the new business environment. In many parts of the USA, there was more than an element of the Wild West. Conmen, thieves and swindlers came to the new towns that were appearing, looking for suitable victims. A second major disadvantage was that Coke was originally a patent medicine and only about 2% of the medicines that were produced ever became well-known – most inventors and salesmen failed miserably. Thirdly, although large profits could be made from all kinds of medicines, many of which often cost almost nothing to produce, by the late 1880s, the market for medicines was already saturated. Patent medicines, therefore, were not an easy commercial area to break into.

4. Another important aspect of the story is that the world of medicine was not advanced at this time. Nineteenth-century American doctors were not numerous, nor were they very good (anaesthetics were still to be invented and some of the primitive methods used by the medical profession were terrifying, killing more patients than they saved). This was the reason why many people turned to alternative remedies, the so-called patent medicines, to solve their health problems. By the end of the century, there were thousands of cures on offer for every imaginable ailment, from the common cold to malaria, all of which required extensive advertising in newspapers and public places to promote their superior values over their competitors.

5. To conclude, it is not surprising that many would-be tycoons were attracted by the rising numbers of consumers, and that the field of patent medicines was an attractive starting point for some. In 1869, Dr John Pemberton, a Georgia pharmacist, had moved to Atlanta searching to make his fortune by the discovery of the perfect patent cure. In 1886, after long years of research, he finally launched his new invention. It was into this very crowded and over-competitive market that Coca-Cola was to emerge as a highly successful product.

Task 2 Linking words and phrases

2.1 Individual work

Students follow instructions in the Student's Book. After correcting the activity, ask students why the essay writer chose to use the sequencing phrases in preference to firstly, secondly, etc.

Answers:

a. Firstly = The <u>first</u> episode
b. Secondly = <u>One</u> of the most important changes
c. Thirdly = There were, <u>however</u>, some <u>disadvantages</u>
d. Fourthly = <u>Another</u> important aspect
e. Finally = <u>To conclude</u>

2.2 Individual work/Pairwork

Students follow instructions in the Student's Book.

Answers:

a. showing similarity – in the same way; like
b. comparing or contrasting – on the other hand; despite
c. adding something – equally important; another important aspect
d. giving reasons – because of; due to; since
e. showing cause and effect – as a result; therefore
f. giving an example – as shown by; for instance

After you have clarified the answers to the question, you could ask students to add further linkers to each list by brainstorming with a partner.

Task 3 The topic sentence and supporting sentences

3.1 Pairwork

Students follow instructions in the Student's Book.

Answer:
c

3.2 Small group work

Students follow instructions in the Student's Book.

Answer:
Paragraph A is a better-formed paragraph because it develops the idea stated in the topic sentence. In contrast, Paragraph B tends to digress from the topic sentence statement (challenges for incoming families) into an argument about the human rights of incomers.

3.3 Individual work

Responses here will vary. It is a good idea to take this work in and check it.

Answers:
Answers will vary from student to student.

Task 4 Organising an essay

4.1 Individual work/Pairwork/Small group work

Students follow the instructions in the Student's Book.

Answers:

paragraph begins	topic	order
Another important aspect of the story is that the world of medicine was not advanced at this time.	the world of medicine	4
There were, however, some disadvantages to the new business environment.	disadvantages to the business environment	3
To conclude, it is not surprising that many would-be tycoons were attracted by the rising numbers of consumers and that the field of patent medicines was an attractive starting point for some.	the field of patent medicines was an attractive one for would-be tycoons	5
One of the most important changes that helped business success was population growth.	population growth	2
The first episode in the Coca-Cola story is an important part of the rise of capitalism in the United States of America.	the rise of capitalism	1

4.2, 4.3 & 4.4 Individual work/Pairwork

After students have discussed *Task 4.2*, the remaining two tasks could be set for homework.

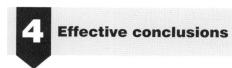

4 Effective conclusions

At the end of this unit, students will be able to:
* write a successful conclusion paragraph

Task 1 Restating the thesis

1.1 Individual work/Pairwork

Students follow instructions in the Student's Book.

Answers:
a.   Fast food and its impact on health in Britain.
     Possible title = Discuss the impact of fast food on health in Britain.
b.   In a similar vein to the introduction, the conclusion states that fast food plays a role in Britons' unhealthy dietary habits. The conclusion adds the idea, however, that increased consumption of fast food is an effect of changes in lifestyle and it is these that underlie the development of an increasingly unhealthy Britain.

1.2 Pairwork

Students follow instructions in the Student's Book.

Possible answers:

original	synonym
lack of	insufficient
consequences	impact
travellers	commuters
major point	main focus
discussed	explored

1.3 Individual work

Students follow instructions in the Student's Book.

Possible answer:
In conclusion, this essay has argued that insufficient investment in public transport is currently having a negative impact on Britain's commuters.

Task 2 Organising the concluding paragraph

2.1 & 2.2 Individual work/Pairwork

Ask students to do this task individually, and then compare their answers with a partner's.

Answers:
2.1
a.   2
b.   1
c.   4
d.   3
e.   5

2.2
a.   b
b.   not given
c.   c
d.   e
This concluding paragraph is effective, but it does not provide a summary of the main points covered in the essay.

Task 3 Finishing with a clear statement

3.1 Individual work

Students follow instructions in the Student's Book.
Feedback could be given by peers or by the tutor.
It may be helpful to elicit a set of criteria for this purpose.

Answers:
Answers will vary from student to student.

3.2 Individual work/Pairwork

This activity could be given to students who finish *Task 3.1* ahead of their classmates. Alternatively, it could be set for homework.

Possible answers:

advantages	disadvantages
• you know the destination of your essay • your conclusion matches your thesis statement	• as you are writing, you may change your argument. If you forget to change your conclusion, it will not match your thesis statement

Task 4 Lecturer expectations

This task could be set for homework. It might form the basis of a tutorial if these feature on your course.

4.1 Individual work

Students follow instructions in the Student's Book.

Answers:
Answers will vary from student to student.

5 Academic style and register

At the end of this unit, students will be able to:
- identify some of the features of academic style
- use formal, objective language
- use cautious language (hedging) to avoid making false claims

Task 1 Formal or informal register?

1.1 &1.2 Individual work/Pairwork

Students follow instructions in the Student's Book.

Possible answers:

feature	formal/written examples
use of contractions: *isn't, don't*, etc.	full forms used, e.g., *would*
use of fillers: *well, er*, etc.	—
use of passive voice	more frequent, e.g., *two main branches may be distinguished*
impersonal and objective	non-use of personal pronouns, e.g., *i; the reader is not mentioned*
personal and subjective	—
punctuation	uses punctuation
imprecise language	avoids imprecision
conciseness	prefers concise forms, e.g., noun phrases for an idea, e.g., *the interrelation of these features*

1.3 Pairwork

Students follow instructions in the Student's Book.

Answers:
a. I
b. F
c. F
d. I
e. F
f. I
g. I
h. I
i. F
j. I
k. I
l. F

Task 2 Cautious language

2.1 Individual work

Students follow instructions in the Student's Book.

Answers:
a. The new vaccine *might* prevent the spread of Ebola.
    40%–49% likely
b. The new vaccine *will probably* prevent the spread of Ebola.
    50%–75% likely
c. The new vaccine *will* prevent the spread of Ebola.
    100% certain

2.2 Individual work

Students follow instructions in the Student's Book.

Answers:
- Statement b is presented as fact.
- Hedging words or expressions used to make the other statements less assertive:
    a. Drinking green tea *appears* to lower the risk of developing cancer.
    b. Some studies *suggest* that drinking green tea *can* lower the risk of developing *certain* cancers.
- *Some studies* distances the writer from the claim.

2.3 & 2.4 Pairwork

Students follow instructions in the Student's Book.

Answers:
2.3
a. Some colleges and universities in this country <u>appear to have</u> large numbers of international students.
b. <u>It could be argued that</u>, instead of coming here, international students should study in their own country.
c. This <u>would seem to be</u> a misapplication of government policy.
d. <u>To a certain extent</u>, this <u>may</u> be true.
e. Erlichman's findings <u>suggest</u> that the amount of independent study <u>might</u> be directly related to higher performance levels.
f. <u>Evidence indicates that</u> inflation will <u>probably</u> not rise next year.
g. The survey <u>tends to indicate</u> that English schoolchildren are <u>apparently</u> not in favour of learning more foreign languages.
h. There are <u>undoubtedly</u> situations where this <u>would seem to be</u> the only <u>possible</u> solution.

2.4

hedging feature	example
hedging verbs	… appear to have… seem suggest tends
use of modal verbs	would might may could
qualifying expressions	To a certain extent, …
probability adjectives and adverbs	probably undoubtedly apparently possible
set expressions	Evidence indicates that … It could be argued that …

Task 3 Register in use

3.1 & 3.2 Individual work/Pairwork

Ask students to complete the task, and then compare their answers with a partner's and then look at the original text in *Unit 3*, *Task 1.2* on page 14 of the Student's Book together to check their work.

Possible answers:
A <u>massive</u> change – <u>one which really helped business – was more people arriving</u> in the USA. <u>There were two times as many people who got here</u> between 1880 and 1910 and <u>lots of them</u> came from <u>all sorts of different places like</u> Europe. If <u>you</u> wanted to be successful <u>you had to work really hard</u>; however, <u>you</u> could get rich quickly if <u>you did this</u>. <u>Lots of</u> immigrants <u>made it</u> and because of this, <u>lots</u> more <u>wannabe</u> millionaires <u>turned up</u> in the <u>US</u>. By 1890, America <u>maybe had around</u> 4,000 millionaires. One of the <u>best</u> was Andrew Carnegie, who <u>got rich</u> through <u>trains and iron and steel</u>. His message was called the 'Gospel of Wealth'.

3.3 Individual work/Pairwork

Ask students to work in pairs to identify inappropriate language and places where hedging would be appropriate.

Possible answer:
A further kind of useful alternative fuel is electricity. At present, this would not seem to be a very efficient fuel, because the technology is somewhat limited; however, it may be argued that recent advances in the production of electric cars could make this a reality in the future. Cars powered with electricity tend to release little or no emissions, so to maximise this benefit it would be advisable to encourage consumers to switch to buying electric cars. Changing consumer preferences may take some time.

 6 Guidelines for the future

At the end of this unit, students will be able to:
*   understand the editing and redrafting process in essay writing
*   understand what lecturers expect from a piece of academic writing

Task 1 Things to remember

1.1 Individual work

Students follow instructions in the Student's Book.

Answers:
Answers will vary from student to student.

Task 2 Redrafting

Ask students to read through the example given in the Student's Book and point out that this feedback is given during the essay drafting process. The essay has not been submitted.

2.1 Individual work

Ask students to guess what *Sp.* and *gr.* mean (*spelling* and *grammar*). Students then follow instructions in the Student's Book.

Possible answer:
According to Thirkell (2007), in 2000, it was forecast that the number of robberies would rise by 29% in London between April 2001 and March 2002, but the actual figures show that the overall number of crimes fell during this period.

2.2 Classwork

Students follow instructions in the Student's Book.

Answers:
a.   Probably a minimum of two.
b.   See table in *Task 2.3*.

2.3 Pairwork/Classwork/Small group work

Students follow instructions in the Student's Book.

Possible answers:

redrafting: things to work on	considerations
paragraphs	• the right structure • each paragraph has a main idea • paragraphs are in the right order
grammar	• articles • sentence grammar • word order • accurate link words
length of essay	• respect the instructions
vocabulary	• accurate use of technical terms
argument	• evidence supports the claim made in a paragraph • the main claims support the thesis statement • the thesis statement is echoed by the summary sentence in the conclusion • the argument is relevant to the question set
sources	• accurate quotations • accurate paraphrasing • adequate and accurate referencing • accurate bibliography
formal style	• impersonal, objective tone • formal vocabulary, e.g., Latinate • full forms • avoids colloquialisms and idiomatic language

Task 3 How to get a better mark

Ask students to look at the example and decide which feedback comments relate to the argument and which to the language. Then ask students to explain each of the comments.

type of feedback	feedback comment	what the comment means
argument	good to include e.g.	The point lacks sufficient substantiation. Add an example.
	ref? – this is rather a generalisation!	The statement is too general to stand without some sort of reference to the literature. Add one or more references and make the statement more specific.
language	Sp.	Spelling: goverment > government

3.1 Classwork

Students follow instructions in the Student's Book.

Answers:
c and f

3.2 Individual work

Students follow instructions in the Student's Book.

Answers:
Answers will vary from student to student.

3.3 Individual work/Pairwork

Students follow instructions in the Student's Book, and then compare their answers with a partner's.

Answers:

marking criteria	mark (%)
ideas generally not made clear and often irrelevant; weak paragraphs; small range of vocabulary; grammatical structure is very limited	40–49
ideas generally clear but not always very relevant; some lack of paragraphing; limited range of vocabulary; limited grammatical structure at times	50–59
lacks any satisfactory organisation or development of ideas; vocabulary use very weak; unsatisfactory use of grammatical structure; generally fails to meet the required pass standard	30–39
excellent text organisation; clear paragraphs with well-expressed ideas; wide range of vocabulary; good use of grammatical structure	70+
good text organisation with generally relevant ideas; adequate range of vocabulary and grammatical structure	60–69

Marking schemes vary from institution to institution. Encourage students to find out about marking schemes in their (future) institution.

Task 4 A model essay

Focus students on the four photos and elicit what they have in common.

4.1 Individual work

Students follow instructions in the Student's Book.

Answers:
Discuss the problems associated with urban overcrowding and evaluate possible solutions.

4.2 Individual work/Pairwork

Ask students to work through the questions individually, and then compare their answers with a partner's.

Answers:
a. The writer arouses interest by underlining the global nature and actuality of the problem.
b. This essay is to identify solutions to some of these problems of urban overcrowding and attempt to evaluate their feasibility.

4.3 Individual work

This task could be set for homework. After students have worked on the task individually, they should compare notes with a partner.

Answers:
Paragraph 1
Topic sentence key words:
Urban overcrowding = has become a global phenomenon
Support examples and evidence:
Rise of megacities – around 20 million population = important trend in last 20 years, e.g., New York

Paragraph 2
Topic sentence key words:
Reasons for megacities' growth: economic security + improved social conditions
Support examples and evidence:
Cities develop as economic centres, e.g., post-World War II megacities: Sydney, Sao Paulo + Frankfurt; Tokyo – expanded in line with the city's economic growth

Paragraph 3
Topic sentence key words:
No. 1 problem = poverty + inability of developing countries to cope with high population density in cities
Support examples and evidence:
Rural to urban migration: live in shanty towns on edge of city.
Problems: unsanitary living conditions; infectious diseases; access to health care + education

Paragraph 4
Topic sentence key words:
Two main solutions: both relocate urban population outside cities.
Support examples and evidence:
1st solution – resettlement, e.g., Shanghai housing resettlement project – successful re: social + economic benefits BUT not address problem of urban sprawl.

Paragraph 5
Topic sentence key words:
2nd solution = relocation of employers to rural areas
Support examples and evidence:
e.g., brownfield sites in rural areas become business parks – successful in Canada & UK BUT:
1. requires long-term investment by government as people will only relocate if have better housing, education, transport, etc.
2. threat to rural environment according to environmentalists.

4.4 Pairwork

Students follow instructions in the Student's Book.

Answers:
a. Paragraphs 1 and 2
b. Paragraphs 4 and 5
c. Paragraph 3

4.5 Pairwork

Students follow instructions in the Student's Book.

Answers:
a. The suggestion that long-term measures would benefit the lives of all city dwellers.
b. It generalises about the type of solutions that would work well, i.e., long-term ones.

4.6 Individual work/Pairwork

Ask students to work individually, underlining examples of assertive language first. They should compare with a partner and then work as a pair, adding cautious language to the text.

If you have a large class, you could give the pairs a copy of different paragraphs of the text. When each pair has identified overly assertive language and rewritten using cautious language, the pairs could be asked to present their new version to the class, explaining why the changes were made. This works particularly well if you can make the text available on computers, and if you can either project students' work, print it out, or upload it to an online wall, e.g., Padlet.

Answers:
Answers will vary from pair to pair.

Task 5 The problem–solution essay

5.1 & 5.2 Individual work/Pairwork

Students follow instructions in the Student's Book, and then compare their flow charts with a partner's.

Answers:
Situation: Recent evidence confirms that global warming is melting the ice in Antarctica faster than had been previously thought.
Problem: Global economic and ecological impact of rising sea levels, especially in highly populated coastland areas of Asia; erosion of the coastline, flooding and reduction in drinking-water supplies.
Solution: 1. local flood prevention measures;
2. education.
Evaluation: Solution 1 is only useful in the short term. Solution 2 is a long-term one. However, it can only help to minimise the impact, rather than prevent sea levels from rising.

Task 6 Write an essay outline

6.1 Individual work

Students follow instructions in the Student's Book.

6.2 Small group work

Students follow instructions in the Student's Book. The outline could form a wall display, either in the classroom or online, e.g., Padlet.

Unit 1, Task 2.1

See p.30 for instructions.

Identify	Describe items that belong to a particular category.
Analyse	Examine in detail by dividing up into the key components and identify the main points.
Describe	Give the main features, characteristics, or events.
Comment on	Identify the main issues and give an informed opinion.
Compare	Describe the main elements of two or more things to show how they are similar. Possibly explain the consequences of the similarities.
Discuss	Look at the most important aspects or something in a balanced way, e.g., advantages and disadvantages, for and against.
Evaluate	Assess how important or useful something is. It is likely to include both positive and negative points.
Exemplify	Show what something is like, using examples.

Scientific Writing

1 Structure and schedule

At the end of this unit, students will learn how to:
- structure their report and include appropriate scientific report sections
- organise their time appropriately

Task 1 Organising a scientific report

As a lead-in, ask students to discuss what forms scientific communication take and why it is important. Elicit examples of well-known scientific communicators.

1.1 Pairwork/Small group work

As a lead-in to the task, focus students on the visual and ask them to work in pairs discussing what the five sections of a scientific report are. Having elicited the answer to question a, ask students to work in small groups to complete the table.

Answers:

	section		question
1.	Introduction	c.	What is the *background* and *aim* of the investigation?
2.	Materials and Methods	e.	What was *done* in the investigation?
3.	Results	b.	What was *found/discovered*?
4.	Discussion	a.	What do the Results *mean*?
5.	Bibliography	d.	What literature *sources* are referenced in the report?

1.2 Classwork

Ask students to give reasons for their answers. If students have had experience of writing scientific reports, ask them to give examples from their own writing.

Task 2 Organising your time

2.1 Individual work/Pairwork

Ask students to work individually, putting the stages in order, and then compare their answers with a partner's. This should take about ten minutes. Encourage students to share their ideas in a brief class discussion.

Possible answers:
1. Complete practical laboratory work.
2. Write first draft of the *Material and Methods* section
3. Write first draft of the *Results* (do calculations, draw up tables, graphs, charts)
4. Research background information
5. Start *Bibliography*
6. Write first draft of the *Discussion*
7. Write first draft of the *Introduction*
8. Give first draft to another student to review using list of 'Points to check'
9. Meet with another student to discuss peer review (have a writing conference)
10. Revise first draft
11. Hand in revised draft

2.2 & 2.3 Individual work/Small group work

Ask students to fill in the table individually, and then compare their answers in small groups. Answers will vary.

Answers:
Possible timetable:

time frame	activity	reason
Day 0	Complete practical laboratory work.	Lab work is fun!
Day 1	Write first draft of *Material and Methods* section. Write first draft of *Results* (do calculations, draw up tables, graphs, charts).	The laboratory work is still fresh in your mind and you need time to complete all the parts of the report before submission.
Day 2	Research background information. Start *Bibliography*. Write first draft of the *Discussion*. Write first draft of the *Introduction*.	You need to know the background literature before writing the *Discussion* and *Introduction*. Writing your Bibliography as you go along will save time, and make errors less likely.
Day 3	Revise first draft.	Taking a break between writing the first draft and revising it allows you to view it more critically/objectively.
Day 4	Give first draft to a classmate to review using list of 'Points to check'.	Peer review can be helpful.
Day 5	Meet with classmate to discuss peer review (have a writing conference).	Discussion with your classmate allows you to explain what you intended and for your reviewer to provide feedback.
Day 6	Revise first draft.	Revise as necessary, remembering that you do not have to include all the reviewer's suggestions.
Day 7	Hand in revised draft.	Submitting on time avoids loss of credit through late submission.

Reflect

If appropriate, ask students to start a science writing diary so that they can keep their reflection tasks in one place. If the diary takes an online format, students could save the template they produce in the diary.

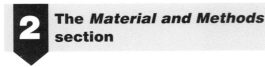

2 The *Material and Methods* section

At the end of this unit, students will:
* review what to include in the *Materials and Methods* section of their report
* learn how and why to write in the passive voice

Task 1 What do I include?

Lead in by asking students why they would start the report writing process with the *Materials and Methods* section.

1.1 & 1.2 Pairwork

Ask students to work in pairs, answering the two questions.

Answers:
1.1
What did you do in your experiment?
1.2
The laboratory work is still fresh in your mind and you need time to complete all the parts of the report before submission.

1.3 & 1.4 Small group work/Classwork

Ask each group to choose a secretary, whose role is to make a note of the main points raised in the discussion. The remaining students should discuss the two questions. Ask each group secretary to report back on the discussion and collect ideas on the board. At this point, students should make a record of the discussion in their Student's Books.

Answers:

include ...	do not include ...
• temperature (air, water) • volume of materials used • mass of materials used • concentrations of solutions • pH • type of microscopy • sampling techniques • species name of organism • age of organisms used • size of organisms used	• information that is common knowledge to the scientific audience reading the report, e.g.: • detailed descriptions of conventional laboratory glassware • detailed descriptions of conventional laboratory techniques

1.5 Individual work

Students work individually to answer T/F/D questions.

Answers:
a. F
b. F
c. T
d. F

Task 2 How do I write a good *Materials and Methods* section?

One possible lead-in is to focus students' attention on the visual and ask them to identify which document is a report and which document is a laboratory schedule.

2.1 Individual work/Pairwork

Refer students back to the example report and schedule. Ask them to complete the task individually, and then compare their answers with a partner's.

Answers:
Laboratory schedules are usually written in the <u>imperative</u> as a list of instructions. However, when you write your report, you must summarise what you did in full <u>sentences</u> and well-developed <u>paragraphs</u>. You will usually write in the <u>past</u> tense and use the <u>passive</u> voice.

2.2 Classwork

Ask students to think about any reports they have written previously. Did these reports have a similar style?

Then ask students to consider the questions asked in the Student's Book.

Answers:
a. A *schedule* is a set of instructions to follow (a protocol) in order to complete an analytical procedure. A *report* explains what you did and why.
b. Paragraphs are used to separate and organise ideas and to provide clarity.
c. The passive is common as it focuses the reader's attention on *what* was done rather than on *who* did it.

2.3 Classwork

As a lead-in to this task, if appropriate, ask students to read the two sentences, underlining active verbs and circling passive ones.

Answer:
b

Task 3 Using the passive

3.1 Individual work

Ask students to read the example, and deduce the rule for the passive form.

Answers:
The object in the active sentence, *the analysis*, becomes the <u>subject</u> in the passive sentence. The subject in the active sentence, *John*, changes position in the passive sentence as it comes <u>after</u> the main verb and is introduced with <u>by</u>.

3.2 Individual work

Ask students to read the example and explanation, and deduce the rule for the passive form of verbs that take two objects. In the feedback stage of the activity, students may ask how they should decide which of the two objects to put in the subject position.

Answers:

In the active sentence above, the two objects are the caterpillars and one dose. One or the other can become the subject in the passive sentence.

3.3 Individual work/Pairwork

Ask students to complete the passive form individually, and then compare their answers with a partner's.

Answers:

Past simple

The plant was taken.   The plants were taken.
A pot was made.   The pots were made.
The image was shown.   The images were shown.

Past perfect

The solution had been shaken.   The solutions had been shaken.
The animal had been fed.   The animals had been fed.
The mixture had been kept.   The mixtures had been kept.

Past continuous

A record was being made.   Records were being made.
An attachment was being fitted. Attachments were being fitted.
The result was being analysed. The results were being analysed.

3.4 Small group work

Focus students' attention on the graphic and the tutor's feedback at the end of the *Materials and Methods* section. Ask each group of students to work through the text three times, first identifying how to focus the reader on the method, second looking at improving the paragraphing and finally underlining all the nouns. Students should make a note of their discussions.

3.5 Individual work/Pairwork

This task could be set for homework.

Possible answers:

Field work recordings were started on 12 February, 2014, and ended on 12 March, 2014. A digital camera was used to record the animals found on the beach and animals were marked with quick-drying, non-toxic paint. Recordings of environmental conditions, including temperature, salinity and substrate, were being made at the same time.
Laboratory experiments were begun at the same time as the field work. Each day ten animals were collected from the beach and placed in controlled conditions in the laboratory until experiments began.
The apparatus was set up as shown in Figure 1 and one crab was placed in each specimen tube. By the time an experiment started, the crabs had been acclimatised for at least two days and had been fed daily. Food had been prepared in advance.
At the end of each experiment, a digital camera was used to record the animals' appearance. Photographs taken at the beach had been printed for comparison. The results were being analysed continuously. Results were analysed using statistical tests.

For your feedback session on this task, the activity on page 50 can be photocopied onto card and cut up. Ask students to rearrange the paragraphs in the correct order and then decide whether the missing verbs should be active or passive and what the tense should be.

Paragraph order spells: FIELD

The missing verbs are underlined in the possible answers for *Task 3.5*.

Reflect

If students would benefit from further practice, refer them to the reflection activity on page 8 of the Student's Book.

3 The *Results* section

At the end of this unit, students will:

- review what to include in the *Results* section
- learn how to present and describe tables and figures
- be able to write about their results

Task 1 What to include

1.1 & 1.2 Individual work

Ask students to recall what question the *Results* section of a report answers (*Task 1.1*).

Answer:

1.1
What was found/discovered?

1.2
a. histogram
b. table
c. line graph
d. pie chart

1.3 Pairwork

Students follow instructions in the Student's Book.

Answers:

a. A *figure* is a graphical representation of the data, a *table* is the data itself.
b. Tables/figures should be included as they clarify/simplify results.
a. Table – title above; figure – title below.
b. Labels, titles.

Task 2 Preparing tables and graphs

2.1 Pairwork

Students follow instructions in Student's Book.

Answers:
a. • Table 1 lists points of comparison across the top of the table and species down the side. Table 2 does the reverse.
   • Table 1 gives units of measurement for the points of comparison, while Table 2 does not.
   • Table 1 gives the date when the data were collected; Table 2 does not.
   • Table 2 uses abbreviations inconsistently, e.g., Av./Aver.
b. Table 1
c. It would not be better to show this data in a graph. It would be better in a table.

2.2 Small group work

Students follow instructions in the Student's Book. At the end of the activity, introduce/recycle the vocabulary **independent variable** and **dependent variable** in preparation for the following activity.

Possible answers:
• Data for a particular characteristic are arranged vertically, rather than horizontally.
• Each column heading is followed by the units.
• Numbers in a column are aligned.
• Only acceptable abbreviations are used.
• The table has a number (Arabic) and a title.
• The title is complete and allows the reader to understand the essence of the table without referring to the text.

2.3 Individual work/Pairwork

Ask students to discuss the questions in pairs and then draw their graphs individually. When they have finished, they should compare their work with a partner's.

Answers:

strengths	weaknesses
• most of the data are accurately represented	• the independent data are on the y-axis • not all axes are labelled • data not always accurately represented

2.4 Individual work/Pairwork

Ask students to discuss the questions in pairs and then draw their graphs individually. When they have finished, they should compare their work with their partner's.

Answer:

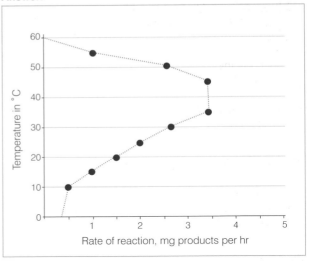

Task 3 Writing the text of the *Results* section

3.1 Individual work/Pairwork

Ask students to look at the sample paragraph and find examples of:
a. use of past tense in the active voice
b. a general statement describing an important finding
c. data that support the general statement

Answers:
a. varied/was/increased/decreased/was
b. Oxygen production varied depending on the pH of the solution.
c. At pH 2, oxygen production was 3 ml, whereas at pH 7 it increased to a maximum of 6 ml. At pH values above 7, oxygen production decreased and was at a minimum of 1 ml at pH 10.

3.2 Individual work/Pairwork

Ask students to work with a partner identifying findings and supporting evidence in order to develop a paragraph. Students then work individually to write a paragraph.

3.3 Small group work

Ask students to work together to identify the main features of a good description of results. On the basis of this list, they should brainstorm advice for writing a *Results* section.

Reflect

If appropriate, ask students to add the reflection task to their science writing diary.

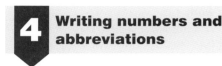

4 Writing numbers and abbreviations

At the end of this unit, students will:
- understand when to use numerals and spell numbers in scientific reports
- familiarise themselves with the conventions for using abbreviations

Task 1 Writing numbers

1.1 Pairwork

Put students into pairs. Ask them to read the guidelines to find examples of numerals, ordinals, fractions and decimal forms and then to check with their partners.

Possible answers:
a.   a numeral = 2
b.   an ordinal = seventh
c.   a fraction = a third
d.   a decimal form = 0.5

Then ask students to explain the terms **numeral** and **ordinal** to their partners without looking back at the Student's Book. When they have finished, they should check their work against the explanations given on page 13 of the Student's Book.
a numeral = used to express *quantities* and *mathematical relationships*
an ordinal = number that conveys order or rank
Then elicit explanations of **fraction** and **decimal form**.

1.2 Individual work/Pairwork

Ask students to work through the task individually, referring back to the guidelines to help them. They should compare their answers with a partner's and be prepared to explain them.

Answers:
a.   3
b.   5
c.   4
d.   1
e.   2

1.3 Individual work

Students follow instructions in Student's Book.

Answers:
a.   Experiments lasting 1 day indicated that the temperature was one of the most important factors, whereas 7-day toxicity tests suggested that salinity was crucial.
b.   Five gammarus were placed in 50 ml of 0%, 50% and 100% sea water solutions.
c.   The animals were collected at Swansea Bay and one half were divided between three 50 ml pots.
d.   After washing twice in buffer, the tissue was immersed in 2% osmium tetroxide in 0.25 M phosphate buffer, for 1 hr.

Task 2 Common scientific abbreviations

2.1 Classwork

If you think your class will be familiar with most of the abbreviations, this activity could be turned into a competition, with the two halves of the class competing to find the full forms of the abbreviations. When this is finished, ask students to complete the task in writing.

Alternatively, if you think your students will be unfamiliar with the abbreviations, this activity could be turned into a vocabulary snowball activity, using the table on page 51. Photocopy the table and cut up the abbreviations. Give each student an abbreviation and ask him/her to read it, check any unknown vocabulary in a dictionary, and then learn the abbreviation. Students should then move around the classroom, teaching their abbreviation to a classmate, who reciprocates. When both students have finished explaining their abbreviation, the pair swaps abbreviations. Each student then looks for a new classmate to teach his/her abbreviation to, swapping abbreviations again, and so on until the whole group has learned all of them. If you have fewer than 12 students in the group, feed in new abbreviations to replace ones that everyone has learned. At the end of the activity, ask students to complete *Task 2.1* on page 14 of the Student's Book.

Answers:
a.   s = second(s)
b.   min = minute(s)
c.   h/hr = hour(s)
d.   g = gram(s)
e.   mg = milligram(s)
f. μm = micrometer(s)/micron(s)
g.   O = oxygen
h.   MW = molecular weight
i.   U = atomic mass point
j.   bp = boiling point
k.   DNA = deoxyribonucleic acid
l.   UV = ultraviolet

Task 3 Using numbers and abbreviations in the *Results* section

3.1 Individual work/Pairwork/Classwork/Larger group work/Small group work/Plenary

Possible answers:
a.   Table should be reversed: Columns should be Pond A and Pond B. Rows should be *Daphnia magna* and *Cyclops bicuspidatus*.
b.   Inconsistent expression of numbers; numbers should express decimals to the same number of places and be aligned. Units should be included in each heading: Cadmium(μg l^{-1}) and Zinc (μg l^{-1})
c.   Names should be written in full.
d.   Title should give full details (it correctly appears above the table).
e.   Use past tense in description of what the effects were, e.g., … the toxicity of cadmium was greater than for zinc.
f.   General statements should be supported with data from the table.

3.2 Individual work

This task could be set for homework.

Possible answers:
Table 3: Seven-day LC50 values for cadmium and zinc for
Daphnia magna and Cyclops bicuspidatus collected from Pond
A and Pond B

	Pond A	Pond A	Pond B	Pond B
	Cadmium (μg l^{-1})	Zinc (μg l^{-1})	Cadmium (μg l^{-1})	Zinc (μg l^{-1})
Daphnia magna	296	5000	23	490
Cyclops bicuspidatus	3800	5500	320	520

Table 3 shows the Seven-day LC50 values (concentrations at
which half the sample dies after seven days) for cadmium and
zinc for populations of *Daphnia magna* and *Cyclops bicuspidatus*
collected from Pond A and from Pond B.

The results indicate that for both *D. magna* and *C. bicuspidatus*
the toxicity of cadmium was greater than for zinc, for example,
the Seven-day LC50 value for *D. magna* from Pond A was 296
μg l^{-1} for cadmium compared with 5000 μg l^{-1} for zinc. Similarly,
for *C. bicuspidatus* from Pond A, the Seven-day LC50 value was
3800 μg l^{-1} for cadmium compared with 5500 μg l^{-1} for zinc.

The results also indicate that animals collected from Pond B
were more sensitive to cadmium and zinc poisoning them those
collected from Pond A. For example, the Seven-day LC50 value
for *D. magna* from Pond B was 23 μg l^{-1} cadmium compared with
296 μg l^{-1} cadmium for *D. magna* from Pond A.

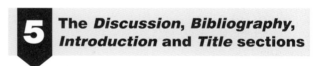

5 The *Discussion, Bibliography, Introduction* and *Title* sections

At the end of this unit, students will:
- review what to include in the *Discussion* section of
  a report
- learn how to cite references and write a *Bibliography*
- be able to write an appropriate *Introduction* and *Title*

Task 1 What to include in the *Discussion*

Ask students to recall what question the *Material and
Method* and *Results* sections answered.

1.1 Individual work

Now ask what question the *Discussion* section answers.

Answer:
What do the results mean?

1.2 Small group work

Encourage students to discuss the table of results
together and make a note of their questions.

Possible answers:
- Are there any significant differences in overall beetle
  numbers in the two locations?
- Are there any significant differences in the numbers of
  species found in the two locations?
- Are there any differences in the beetle assemblages?
- Are there more species that are rare/of conservation
  importance in one wood compared to the other?

1.3 Individual work/Pairwork

Students follow instructions in the Student's Book, and
then compare their answers with a partner's.

Answers:
The *Discussion* section of the report will generally move from the
specific (the results of your experiment) to the general (how your
results fit in with other scientific findings).
Normally, the Discussion should do the following:
- Explain whether your results support your original
  hypothesis.
- Consider any surprising data or deviations from what you
  expected.
- Consider sources of error.
- Consider improvements in experimental method.
- Relate your findings to previous results in the same area
  and derive conclusions about the process you are studying.
- Look at the practical and theoretical implications of your
  findings.
- Make suggestions for extensions of your study.

1.4 Individual work/Pairwork

Students follow instructions in the Student's Book, and
then compare their answers with a partner's.

Answers:
a. All the elements are included.
b. Underlining could include the following:
The results show that populations of common beetle
species were similar in both woodlands and were
comparable to numbers found in previous studies. These
common beetles are found in most woodland habitats.
As expected, it was also found that the diversity of beetle
species was higher in Peasemore Wood than in Hailey
Wood. Peasemore Wood was found to contain a high
number of beetle species which are rare in the UK.
The results show that for beetles, Peasemore Wood is of
more conservation interest than Hailey Wood. It is a suitable
habitat for some beetle species which are rare in Britain and
are identified in species recovery plans that aim to increase
their numbers in UK habitats. Peasemore Wood, therefore,
should take priority in management and investment for
beetle conservation purposes over Hailey Wood.
However, this data does not show the overall biodiversity
of either of the woodlands. There may be other species of
conservation importance present in Hailey Wood that have
not been recorded in this study. Therefore, further work
should be carried out to assess the overall biodiversity of
both of these woodlands before any decisions regarding
management or investment are made for either.

Task 2 Citing references and writing a bibliography

Point out to students that they should find out which referencing system they are required to use on their programme/module.

2.1 Individual work/Pairwork

Ask students to work individually to work out the order of information rule, and then ask them to compare their answer with a partner's.

Answer:
Author, A.A. (Date of publication). *Title* (XX ed.). Location: Publisher.

2.2 & 2.3 Individual work/Pairwork

Ask students to work through the questions individually, and then compare their answers with a partner's.

Answers:
a. 33 = volume number and *18661–18671* = page numbers
b. (*Euro*) *J. Neurosci* = (*European*) *Journal of Neuroscience* (and the given names of the authors)
c. The first citation is a print journal, while the second is an electronic journal.

Task 3 What to include in the *Introduction*

3.1 Small group work

Now ask what questions the *Introduction* section answers.

Answers:
What is the background to this study?
What is the aim?

3.2 Small group work

Students complete the True/False activity.

Answers:
a. F
b. F
c. T
d. T
e. F

3.3 Small group work

Ask students to reorganise the sentences to make an introductory text. Alternatively, there is a photocopiable activity on page 52.

Answers:
4
1
5
3
2
6

Review the task by eliciting from students a likely order of information:
*   Start with a general statement relating to the topic under investigation.
*   Move on to the specific focus of the study.
*   Provide background information from the literature (cite references).
*   Identify unanswered questions or inconsistencies.
*   State the aim and objectives of the current study.

Task 4 What makes a good *Title*?

4.1 & 4.2 Small group work/Classwork

After students have discussed which title is better and why in small groups, collect ideas together as a class.

Answers:
Title b is better because it gives the reader a more complete description of the study.
Title a is too general; the second includes important key words and phrases (temperature, oxygen consumption, mice).

4.3 Pairwork/Classwork

Ask pairs of students to discuss this question. Ask them to write down, in note form, their conclusions about what makes a title appropriate. Encourage pairs to feed back to the class, explaining why elements are necessary.

Answers:
a. Title 1 provides the required information, including key words and phrases (summer phytoplankton; Lake Windermere).
b. Title 2 provides the required information, including key words and phrases.

Reflect

When your students have completed the reflection activity, you could ask them to share their templates with each other to collect useful ideas of information to include in the template.

Ask students to bring a corrected piece of their scientific writing to the next class.

6 Editing and revising your report

At the end of this unit, students will:
- understand how to check their work for grammatical and vocabulary mistakes
- practise editing their work to ensure they use full sentences that are clear and concise

Task 1 What do I check for?

As a lead-in, focus students on the visual and elicit what 'Sp.' stands for and what correction needs to be made.

1.1 & 1.2 Individual work/Pairwork

Ask students to fill in the table, referring to the piece of work they brought along to class if they did so, and then think of other problem areas.

Task 2 Use of tenses

2.1 & 2.2 Individual work/Pairwork

Ask students to work through the tasks individually and then check their answers to *Task 2.1* by looking back through the previous units in the Student's Book, before discussing their answers in pairs.

Answers:
2.1
a. was
b. presents
c. is
d. varied
e. found
f. is; results
2.2
Sentence a uses the passive. It is in the *Materials and Methods* section – who did an action is unimportant information. The focus is on what happened.

Task 3 Common mistakes with vocabulary

3.1 Individual work/Larger group work

This task could be copied onto a presentation slide/IWB and initially completed as a team competition, before students complete the task in the book.

Answers:
a. **1.** affects
       2. effect
b. **1.** continuous
       2. continual
c. **1.** cites
       2. site
d. **1.** there
       2. their

3.2 & 3.3 Individual work/Pairwork

Elicit the differences between the pairs of words before students start writing their pairs of sentences.
a.   Fewer + countable noun/less + uncountable noun
b.   breath = noun/breathe = verb
c.   rise = intransitive verb/raise = transitive verb
d.   consecutive = one after another without interruption/ concurrent = happening at the same time

Students' sample sentences could be collected together on the board and then the class could vote for the best ones. Alternatively, students could write out their sentences omitting the key words, and swap them with a partner, who then completes the sentences.

Task 4 Plurals

Ask students if there are nouns whose plural forms they tend to hesitate over.

4.1 Individual work/Larger group work

This task could be copied onto a presentation slide/IWB and initially completed as a team competition, before students complete the task in the book.

Answers:

singular	plural
analysis	analyses
bacterium	bacteria
criterion	criteria
datum	data*
formula	formulae/formulas
hypothesis	hypotheses
medium	media
ratio	ratios
phenomenon	phenomena

Note: *You might like to draw students' attention to 'data', which was a plural form traditionally, but can be used as a singular.*

4.2 Individual work

After students have worked through the task individually, elicit further examples of words following the rule.

Answers:
a.   Greek or Latin-based singular nouns that end in ~*um* generally form the plural by changing ~*um* to ~*a*.
a.   Greek or Latin-based singular nouns that end in ~*is* generally form the plural by changing ~*is* to ~*es*.

4.3 Individual work/Pairwork

Ask students to underline the subject head noun in each sentence and then check the number in the verb. They should compare their answers with a partner's.

Answers:
a. This <u>data</u> is/These <u>data</u> **are** supported by evidence from other studies.
b. Ten <u>drops</u> of hydrochloric acid were added to each sample.
c. The <u>period</u> of immersion for crabs at different times of the tidal cycle ~~are~~ **is** presented in Table 1.
d. One <u>source</u> of error in these experiments ~~are~~ **is** the inaccuracy in recording light intensities.

Task 5 Be clear and concise

Elicit how being concise leads to clarity.

5.1 Pairwork/Small group work

Students follow instructions in the Student's Book.

Possible answers:
a. The zooplankton were affected by pH.
b. The experiments alone cannot indicate the optimum conditions.
c. 50 ml aliquots 0%, 5%, 10%, 15%, 20%, 25%, 30%, 35%, 40%, 45% sodium chloride solutions were placed in test tubes.

Task 6 Write in complete sentences

6.1 Pairwork/Small group work

Students follow instructions in the Student's Book. After correcting the task, elicit the main points to check in terms of complete sentence structures. If students have a corrected piece of writing to hand, ask them to find examples of incomplete sentence structures in their own work and correct them.

Possible answers:
a. In the third set of experiments, citric acid concentration was doubled and at each temperature three sets of readings. *In the third set of experiments, the concentration of citric acid was doubled and three sets of readings were taken at each temperature.*
b. Enzymes are denatured at high temperatures. Because molecular conformation is altered. *Enzymes are denatured at high temperatures because molecular conformation is altered.*
c. The reaction occurred at its maximum; copper was absent. *The reaction occurred at its maximum when copper was absent.*

Task 7 Write well-constructed paragraphs

7.1 Pairwork/Small group work

Students follow instructions in the Student's Book. If students have a piece of their writing to hand, after correcting the task, ask them to apply the true statements to a paragraph they have written.

Answers:
a. T
b. T
c. F
d. F
e. T

Unit 2, Task 3.5

See page 43 for instructions.

L	At the end of each experiment, a digital camera _____ (*use*) to record the animals' appearance. Photographs taken at the beach had been printed for comparison. The results _____ (*analyse*) continuously.
D	Results _____ (*analyse*) using statistical tests.
I	Laboratory experiments _____ (*begin*) at the same time as the field work. Each day ten animals were collected from the beach and placed in controlled conditions in the laboratory until experiments _____ (*begin*).
F	Field work recordings _____ (*start*) on 12 February 2014 and ended on 12 March 2014. A digital camera was used to record the animals found on the beach and animals were marked with quick-drying, non-toxic paint. Recordings of environmental conditions, including temperature, salinity and substrate, _____ (*make*) at the same time.
E	The apparatus was set up as shown in Figure 1 and one crab was placed in each specimen tube. By the time an experiment started, the crabs had been acclimatised for at least two days and _____ (*feed*) daily. Food had been prepared in advance.

Unit 4, Task 2.1

See page 45 for instructions.

s = second(s)	O = oxygen
min = minute(s)	MW = molecular weight
h/hr = hour(s)	U = atomic mass unit
g = gram(s)	bp = boiling point
mg = milligram(s)	DNA = deoxyribonucleic acid
μm = micrometer(s)/micron(s)	UV = ultraviolet

Unit 5, Task 3.3

See page 47 for instructions.

1	Woodland habitats have been in decline throughout Britain for centuries. This decline has been most notable since the Industrial Revolution and the mechanisation of farming practices.
2	With the decline in woodland, many organisms are under threat from a loss of habitat.
3	The organisms under most threat are the plants and the insects. These organisms tend to have low dispersal rates and are slow to colonise new habitats. Many species of plants and invertebrates are now threatened with extinction in Britain due to a loss of habitat.
4	Many of these species are the subject of species recovery plans designed to manage suitable habitat and increase their numbers. Organisations with responsibilities for areas of woodlands are often lacking in sufficient resources to protect the entire woodland habitat under their jurisdiction.
5	Therefore, they have to prioritise woodlands that are in need of immediate protection.
6	This study assesses the importance of two woodland habitats to beetle conservation.

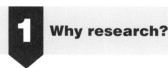

Module 6 Research & Online Sources

1 Why research?

At the end of this unit, students will be able to:
- recognise how research can develop their understanding of a topic
- understand the need to refer to sources in their academic work
- have an awareness of different conventions and attitudes to research in different cultures

Task 1 Why research?

1.1 Small group work

If your students use English as an additional language, you may need to pre-teach the term **obesity**.

1.2 Classwork

You could conclude the discussion by pointing out that, without research, an essay relies on the 'common sense' knowledge of the student. This often results in a limited argument or mistruth.

Task 2 Supporting evidence and arguments

2.1 Individual work

If your students use English as an additional language, you may need to pre-teach (some of) the following vocabulary:
a pressing problem
to target
the root causes (of a problem)
the symptoms (of a problem)
to combat (a problem)
a promotional campaign
a well-balanced diet
dairy foods
eliminate (a problem)

Answers:
a.   Not given – note the text merely states that obesity is 'one of the most pressing problems facing the developed world today', and that 'there has been a dramatic rise in the number of obese people', but does not offer any facts or figures to support this statement.
b.   'It is generally caused by poor eating habits, most especially the overconsumption of fast food, salt and sugar.'
c.   Governments could:
  • 'engage in promotional campaigns in schools'
  • 'teach them about the advantages of a well-balanced diet'
  • 'require that the food offered in schools meets minimum health standards'
  • 'eliminate the sale and marketing of unhealthy food'
d.   These steps are effective as they are intended to 'target the root causes of this problem, rather than just its symptoms'.

2.2 Small group work

Students follow instructions in the Student's Book.

Answers:
Answers will vary from student to student.

2.3 Individual work/Pairwork

If students find this task difficult, you may need to work as a class to identify claims made in the essay and check if there is any substantiation provided for the claims.

Answers:
Answers will vary from student to student.
Possible answers are:
(**a** = Add an example.)
(**b** = Add a standard definition as a quotation and/or reference to a relevant current theory.)
(**c** = Add a reference to a relevant theory.)
One of the most pressing problems facing the developed world today is that of obesity. [a] In recent years, there has been a dramatic rise in the number of obese people. This has been accompanied by an associated increase in health problems such as diabetes, heart disease and stroke. It is essential that governments take action and that they target the root causes of this problem rather than just its symptoms. Promoting healthy eating in school will be key in combating obesity.
[b] Obesity is defined as having too much body fat. It is generally caused by poor eating habits, most especially the over consumption of fast food, salt and sugar.
[c] A healthy diet is of utmost importance to all age groups, but especially children and teenagers. Governments should, therefore, engage in promotional campaigns in schools to target young people and teach them about the advantages of a well-balanced diet. School lessons could explain the advantage of eating a variety of different foods, including plenty of fruit and vegetables, some protein, some dairy foods, and only a very small amount. Governments can also require that the food offered in schools meets minimum health standards and they can eliminate the sale and marketing of unhealthy food. Too many school cafeterias currently sell junk food to young people. If this situation is allowed to continue, young people's obesity rates will not decline.

2.4 Pairwork

It is probably best to set *Task 2.4a*, correct the task as a class, and then move on to *Task 2.4b*.

Answers:
a.   • factual information
  • statistics
  • diagrams
  • graphs
  • examples
  • relevant theories
  • quotations from experts
  • experimental data
b.   Answers will vary from student to student.

Task 3 Academic conventions for research

3.1 Individual work/Pairwork

If your students use English as an additional language, it may be useful to pre-teach the following vocabulary:
bibliography
quotation
in-text reference

Answers:
a. Answers will vary from student to student.
b. Kris: Writing is far more prominent as a form of assessment in the UK than in universities in Kris's country.
   Bo: There is a much greater reference to the Literature in the UK than in universities in Bo's country, and so reports in the UK are much longer too.
   Edward: There is a much greater need for personal, unguided research on the part of the essay writer in UK universities.
   Phan: In the UK, it is not sufficient to write a bibliography – in-text references are also required. Also, in the UK, all source material should appear in the bibliography.
c. Some students like the UK system, e.g., Kris, whereas others don't, e.g., Bo.
d. Answers will vary from student to student.

Task 3.1d could be extended into a piece of writing, or form the basis for a role play.

2 The research process

At the end of this unit, students will:
• be able to prepare appropriate research questions
• identify different types of research (primary, secondary)
• be aware of the range of the different sources of information available and their usefulness
• be able to document their research by keeping a detailed list of sources

If possible, hold this lesson in a room in or close to the library.

Task 1 Sources of information

If possible take students on a tour of an academic library to show them the many different sources of information and also draw their attention to the library catalogue and databases. Alternatively, bring different sources of information to the classroom.

1.1 Small group work

Students follow instructions in the Student's Book.

Answers:
See the table below for a general picture.

source	strengths	weaknesses
textbooks	• written for students • level of complexity usually identifiable • may be useful for general overview of the topic	• may be too general • may be time consuming to identify useful areas • not immediately accessible
websites	• may be up-to-date • easy to search online • immediately accessible • may be easy to identify usefulness	• may be unreliable • may be subjective • may not be updated • may be non-academic • may not be substantiated
government (or other official) documents	• may be up-to-date • usually immediately accessible online • easy to search online • likely to be detailed • may not provide sources of information	• may be too specific • may be subjective
academic journal articles	• easy to identify whether it is up-to-date and useful • usually immediately accessible online • easy to search online • reliable and peer reviewed	• may be very specialised • may be too detailed • may be too complex
dictionaries & encyclopaedias	• easy to search online • immediately accessible • very specific so ideal for definitions and topic overviews	• likely to be too detailed or complex for anything other than definitions and topic overviews
newspaper or magazine articles	• easy to search online • immediately accessible • straightforward to read • easy to identify whether it is up-to-date	• may be unreliable • may be subjective • may be non-academic • may be unsubstantiated • may not provide references to sources of information
eTextbooks	• easy to search online • immediately accessible • easy to identify whether it is up-to-date • written for students • level of complexity usually identifiable • may be useful for general overview of the topic	• may be too general • may be time consuming to identify useful areas • not possible to print from screen

Depending on the disciplines your students will study in, you may wish to elicit other sources of information.

You should reinforce that some sources are acceptable to use for providing background knowledge in the initial research phase, but should not be included in references/ bibliography. You may need to elicit examples of this type of source.

Task 2 Evaluating sources of information

2.1 Small group work

Students follow instructions in the Student's Book.

Answers:

	text a	text b	text c	text d	text e	text f
type of text	popular newspaper	academic journal	official document (government)	official document (World Health Organisation)	dictionary	academic book
reliability and authority	unreliable	reliable	generally reliable but seek further support	generally reliable but seek further support	reliable	reliable
currency (up to date)						
usefulness (If so, for what?)	no	yes	yes	yes	yes	yes
language (in)formal, (im)personal	informal, may be personal or impersonal	formal, impersonal	formal, impersonal	formal, impersonal	formal, usually impersonal	formal, impersonal

Task 3 Preparing research questions

3.1 Pairwork/Small group work

Ask students to analyse the essay titles, identifying precise questions they would need to research into in order to answer the task.

Answers:
Answers will vary from student to student.

However, it may be worth pointing out the importance of defining terms, e.g., How can 'technology' be defined?

It may also be useful to emphasise that during the research process, students are likely to add research questions to their list.

3.2 Pairwork/Small group work

Students follow instructions in the Student's Book. If they find the task difficult, you may like to write a prompt on the board, e.g., who, which, what, when, why, how.

Answers:
a. Which eating habits cause obesity?
b. Why are these habits a problem?
c. Who do the problems affect?
d. How could governments regulate eating habits?
e. What are the arguments against government regulation?
f. What are the arguments for government regulation?

Task 4 Researching

4.1 Pairwork

Students follow instructions in the Student's Book.

Answers:
a. Effective note-taking is an important practice to master. You have a lot of new knowledge and you need to develop reliable mechanisms for recording and retrieving it when necessary. But note-taking is also a learning process in itself, helping you to process and understand the information you receive.
    Good note-taking:
    *   enables you to avoid unintentional plagiarism
    *   helps you to focus on what is important in what you are reading or hearing
    *   helps you to understand and remember material, and make connections
    *   helps you to structure the assignments you're researching
    *   provides a personal record of what you've learned (more useful than your lecturer's or friends' notes) and records your questions and ideas
    *   sets you up for exam revision
b. You should summarise the main points in your own words; show the relationships between the main points; include illustrations, examples and diagrams which can help to put ideas in a practical context.

c. Make your notes brief and be selective. Keep them well-spaced so you can see individual points and add more details later, if necessary.

d. Your notes should contain bibliographical information to enable you to locate the source again: https://www.reading.ac.uk/internal/studyadvice/StudyResources/Reading/sta-effective.aspx#why.

4.2 Pairwork

Students work together to find two sources relevant to the research question. In addition to the Student's Book task, you may like to ask them to keep notes on the sources they rejected and their reasons for doing so. This information could be shared in an end-of-activity round-up to help students learn how to evaluate the reliability and authority of a source. Alternatively, set this task for homework.

Answers:
Answers will vary from student to student.

Task 5 Types of research

5.1 Individual work

Depending on the needs of your students, you may need to introduce and differentiate the concepts of primary and secondary research before setting the task. Alternatively, this task could be set for homework prior to the lesson.

Answers:
a. P
b. S
c. P
d. S
e. P

5.2 Pairwork

Students follow instructions in the Student's Book.

Answers:
Primary research: c
Secondary research: a, b, c, d, e, f

5.3 Pairwork

Students follow instructions in the Student's Book.

Answers:
Primary research: gather data from students in your university.
Secondary research: review existing research and quote data therein.
Gather primary data by survey, questionnaire, interview, focus group.
Gather secondary data by searching a university library catalogue or online search.

As a round-up to *Task 5*, you might like to ask students why it is useful to identify whether a research question requires primary or secondary research.

3 Finding and evaluating sources online

At the end of this unit, students will be able to:
- understand various types of online sources and their purpose
- evaluate the quality and reliability of online sources
- select online sources for use in research

Task 1 Using the internet for academic research

It is particularly useful for students to have access to the internet for this lesson as it focuses on online research. Given this focus, it may be worth reviewing advantages and disadvantages of online research with your students.

1.1 Small group work

To help students get the most out of their discussions, ask them to reflect on the last one or two pieces of internet-based research they have carried out for questions b and c.

Answers:
Answers will vary from student to student.

1.2 Individual work

This may be a useful moment to introduce the idea that different research engines will produce different numbers of results. You could ask your students to compare the number of results obtained via Google, Google Scholar, Google Books and Yahoo, for example. You may also want to introduce the idea of meta-search engines, e.g., http://www.webcrawler.com/.

Answer:
a. 110,000,000 (at the time of publication using Google).

Task 2 Searching the web

2.1 Individual work/Pairwork

Students should work individually, and then compare their answers with a partner's.

Answers:
a. keywords
b. academic
c. Scholar
d. databases
e. journal
f. subjects

2.2 Pairwork

It could be useful to review the process for defining a research question before moving on to this task. Students follow instructions in the Student's Book.

Answers:
a. This is a two-step process:
    1. Identify the key ideas in the research question: **effect**, **fast-food advertising**, **children.**
    2. Identify synonyms for these key ideas: **effect**/influence; **fast-food**/junk food; **advertising**/advert/advertisement; **children**/young people

b. **AND**: will allow you to narrow your search to find references containing both terms entered. For example, a search for **children AND advertising** will produce fewer, but more relevant, results.
    OR: will help you widen your search to retrieve references containing both terms entered or each term individually. OR can be helpful when searching using synonyms, for example **obese OR overweight.**
    NOT: allows you to exclude a reference that contains a particular term. NOT can be useful when a word has several meanings and you are sure you wish to exclude references to one of these meanings, for example, **oil NOT petroleum** (if you want to focus on other types of oil). With some search engines, such as Google, you will need to use a dash (–) to achieve the same results. NOT should be used with caution as you run the risk of excluding too many results.

c. Placing words or phrases inside quotation marks is helpful in ensuring that the concept will be searched for as one idea. Search results will be limited only to pages that include these exact words in the same order. It is especially useful when searching for terms/ideas using multiple words or for names. For example, you could search for **'junk food'** or **'World Health Organisation'** to narrow your search.

Point out that these search options can be combined. For example, **'World Health Organisation' AND obesity**.

Remind students that it is important to keep meticulous records of their search engines and searches in order to carry out an effective search without wasting time.

Task 3 Evaluating webpages

If you have access to the internet for this lesson, you could direct your students to the website: http://www.cdc.gov/healthyyouth/obesity/facts.htm in order to critically evaluate the website in a realistic way.

3.1 Pairwork

Students follow instructions in the Student's Book.

Answers:
a. Centers for Disease Control and Prevention (CDC)
b. The CDC is a US government agency focusing on protecting public health through disease control and prevention, so obesity is one of its areas of expertise.
c. No bias is apparent on this page.
d. The statistical data is secondary, but references are provided to the primary sources, so readers could access them if they wished.
e. In the graphic, in the Student's Book, the website was last updated on 11 December, 2014.
f. *gov* means governmental agency.

At the end of the task, you could elicit the main criteria for evaluating a source (reviewing and supplementing the criteria given in *Unit 2*, *Task 2.1*). Alternatively, you may want to emphasise the question of bias, in which case, you could ask students to collect examples of bias for homework and share them with the class.

3.2 Individual work/Pairwork

Students follow instructions in the Student's Book.

Answers:
a. 4
b. 3
c. 6
d. 1
e. 2
f. 5

3.3 Pairwork

Students follow instructions in the Student's Book.

Answers:
a. 1. … **ac.uk/library** = a library in a UK educational institution.
    2. A blog (see below).
    3. A list of official publications issued by an organisation.
    4. A wiki (see below).
b. The term **blog** is short for 'weblog'. It usually refers to a type of website or webpage that is updated frequently, with content appearing in chronological order and with an option for readers to leave comments. A blog usually presents personal opinions or experiences. The style tends to be informal, although this is not always the case.
    A **wiki** is a collaborative website that allows visitors/readers to add or change content. Wikipedia is one of the most well-known examples of a wiki.
    The possible disadvantages of blogs and wikis come from the fact that anyone can create a blog or put content on a wiki. It may not always be clear what authority/expertise these authors have, and how reliable or subjective they are. You could refer students back to *Unit 2, Task 1* where they considered the strengths and weaknesses of different sources for academic research.
    It might be useful to engage students in a discussion of the use of Wikipedia after reflecting on the potential disadvantages of wikis. Many lecturers say students should not use it at all for academic research (for the reasons listed above), while some suggest it can be used as a starting point for doing background research on a topic. They would generally agree that they would not want to see references to Wikipedia in an academic essay or report. If you think your students might encounter mixed views on the question of Wikipedia use, you could ask them to carry out an internet search 'how reliable is Wikipedia'.

3.4 Pairwork

Students follow instructions in the Student's Book.

Answer:
Many webpages have an 'About' link that can be clicked on to find out more about the author, publisher or organisation responsible for the content of the page.

Task 4 Practising website evaluation

4.1 Pairwork

Students follow instructions in the Student's Book.

Answers:
Text: The politics of obesity: seven steps to government action
a. Google Scholar
b. The presence of a title, authors and abstract suggests this source comes from a journal.
c. The title suggests it may be relevant.
d. *Health Affairs* is a peer-reviewed academic journal 'of health policy thought and research'.
e. This source was published in 2002 and so may not be completely up to date.
f. Answers will vary, but most important is for students to justify their decisions. The subtitle, 'seven steps to government action', suggests the article may be of value.
Text: Put pictures of fat people on junk food to show …
a. Google
b. The URL indicates the page is provided by the *Daily Mail*, a tabloid paper in the UK.
c. The source addresses the question of the issue of food industry regulation. This would suggest that it is relevant to the essay title.
d. News articles are not usually considered to be completely reliable or authoritative. The sensationalist title also indicates that this is not academic.
e. The source is dated 19 May, 2014 and so it is not completely up to date, especially for a news item.
f. Answers will vary, but most important is for students to justify their decisions and to discuss why/why not. The story might be useful for some background information on government regulation rather than as a source for an academic essay.

4.2 Pairwork

Students follow instructions in the Student's Book.

Answers:
b. The page gives a reference to a journal article.
c. Given that the article appears in a journal entitled *Obesity Reviews*, and makes an evaluation of and recommendations on interventions to promote healthy eating habits, it seems relevant to the essay task.
d. The article on the page is from an academic journal.
e. The article was published in 2010 and so is relatively up to date.
f. Answers will vary, but most important is for students to justify their decisions. It is worth pointing out that there is reference to what the EATWELL project will do, so the article may not provide results.

4 Understanding and using academic books and journals

At the end of this unit, students will:
- understand the importance of the peer review process and its impact on academic journals
- know how to search library databases for academic books and journals
- evaluate the relevance and usefulness of academic books and journals in their research

Task 1 Understanding academic journals

Ask students to find relevant subject guides provided by their university. These highlight the key journals for a discipline and are often available on university library websites.

1.1, 1.2 & 1.3 Pairwork

Students follow instructions in the Student's Book.

Answers:
1.1
a. 2
b. 3
c. 1
d. 2
e. 3
f. 1
1.2
b. The evaluation of scientific, academic or professional work by others working in the same field.
1.3
a. scholars
b. judge
c. valid
d. objective   any order
e. reliable
f. scholarship
g. research

Task 2 Searching library databases for journals

This task could be set for homework if your students have access to a university library database.

2.1 Pairwork

Students follow instructions in the Student's Book.

Answers:
a. Food and Nutritional Sciences
b. 4 – eating and obesity
c. Answers will vary from student to student.

2.2 Pairwork

Remind students that they are looking at the following research question: What eating habits cause obesity?

Answers:
Mood, eating and obesity: the psychological effect of obesity. (2002)
Not relevant.
The effect of eating fast foods on obesity in adolescents (2012)
Yes – it will provide evidence of whether fast food causes obesity.
Eating functional foods to reduce obesity (1998)
Yes – it will provide evidence of food which does not cause obesity.
Evaluating the success of surgery in fast food induced obesity (2004)
Not relevant.
Eating sweets, desserts and childhood obesity (2001)
Yes – it will provide evidence of whether sweet food causes obesity in children.
Challenging obesity: the effect of genetics (1996)
Not relevant.
Obesity and its impact on premature births (2003)
Not relevant.

2.3 Pairwork

Students follow instructions in the Student's Book.

Answer:
Searching an entire database will be more time-consuming than searching within a specific subject's database.

2.4 Pairwork

Students follow instructions in the Student's Book.

Answers:
a. *Obesity … psychology … mood 2002*
    Keywords, year
b. *surgery/obesity. Rushford, E.*
    Keywords, author
c. *AlKhabusi 2009 genetics*
    Author, year, keywords
d. *2004 – obesity – statistics – USA*
    Year, keywords

Task 3 Using abstracts

Ask students to read the list of elements which usually form an abstract and ask them to predict the order they usually appear in.

3.1 Pairwork

Focus students' attention on the abstract and ask them to match each part to one of the elements.

Answers:
a. background
b. thesis statement or aim
c. context of the study
d. method of the research
e. results or findings
f. conclusion

3.2 Pairwork

Students follow instructions in the Student's Book.

Answers:
Answers will vary from student to student, but may include:
*   To evaluate the relevance of the article.
*   To analyse the argument put forward in the article.
*   The context and aim of the research.
*   The main methods used.
*   The most important finding.
*   To judge whether the article is relevant to your research question.

Task 4 Academic books

If appropriate, get students to bring an example of a reading list for their (future) programme with them to class. As a lead-in to the activity, ask students to work in small groups, comparing their reading lists and discussing the following questions:
*   On average, how much reading is required per week for the module?
*   What type of text are you expected to read most often – (chapters in) books, journal articles or online sources?
*   If the reading list has an essential reading section, what type of text appears in it most often – (chapters in) books, journal articles, or online sources?

Set all three parts of *Task 4* to be completed as pairwork. At the end of activity, ask students to summarise the advantages and disadvantages of academic books, academic journals and online material as sources of information for research.

4.1 Pairwork

Students follow instructions in the Student's Book.

Answers:
Books are selected by academic and library staff.

4.2 Pairwork

Students follow instructions in the Student's Book.

Answers:
Answers will vary from context to context, but the most likely responses are a, b and d.

4.3 Pairwork

When setting this task, you may need to clarify with students that the term online sources refers to online material which does not appear in an online academic journal, e.g., websites.

Answers:
a. 1, 2
b. 1, 2
c. 1, 2, 3
d. 3
e. 1, 2
f. 1, 2
g. 1
h. 3
i. 3
j. 1, 2

1 Defining plagiarism

At the end of this unit, students will be able to:
- understand key terminology
- understand what constitutes plagiarism
- discuss why students might plagiarise
- understand what constitutes common knowledge

Task 1 Defining key terminology

1.1 Individual work/Pairwork

Ask students to work on the task individually, and then compare their answers with a partner's. If you think your class will find this task challenging, offer them a choice of two options for each term:

e.g., **in-text referencing**
4. The use of direct and indirect quotes within the text of your document.
OR
1. A list placed at the end of your work of all the resources cited in your work.

Answers:

a.	3	f.	5
b.	4	g.	1
c.	9	h.	7
d.	2	i.	8
e.	6		

Task 2 Defining plagiarism

It may be worth pointing out that definitions of plagiarism are not universal and so students should find out how plagiarism is defined in their own institutions.

2.1 Individual work/Pairwork

Ask students to work on the task individually, and then compare their answers with a partner's.

Answers:

a.	origins	f.	pretence
b.	acknowledge	g.	expressed
c.	communication	h.	Sciences
d.	reproducing	i.	person's
e.	modifications		

2.2 Pairwork

Students follow instructions in the Student's Book. The main point of the task is to expose students to some of the different forms that plagiarism may take and so answers may vary. However, encourage your students to justify their choice of the most serious form of plagiarism as this may give you pointers to what they consider less serious.

Task 3 Why do students plagiarise?

3.1 & 3.2 Pairwork

Students follow instructions in the Student's Book. At the end of the activity, ask students to reflect on what they learned from doing the two tasks.

Answers:
Answers will vary from student to student, but may include:
3.1
- Believing that the language of the original is perfect and so should not be altered
- Not being sure if one has understood the original text completely

3.2
- Working hard to understand someone else's arguments helps you develop your thinking skills and develops your ability to explore another person's view of the world.

Task 4 Identifying common knowledge

Ask students to read the introduction to the task and elicit examples of what might be considered common knowledge in one country or social group, but not in another.

4.1 Individual work/Pairwork

This task is likely to encourage debate amongst the pairs of students. It may be worth clarifying in advance that some disagreement is likely. If they wish to choose 'depends on the discipline (D)' as an answer, encourage them to specify which discipline. Also, if necessary, check that your students understand the term **citation**. At the end of the activity, it may be worth pointing out that if students are in doubt, they are usually better off citing a reference than running the risk of being accused of plagiarism.

Answers:

a.	N
b.	N
c.	D
d.	C/D
e.	N
f.	D
g.	D
h.	C/D
i.	N
j.	N

4.2 Individual work/Pairwork

This task could be set for homework and followed up in the next class. In the feedback stage, ask students to reflect on what they have learned about common knowledge from completing the task.

2 Referencing

At the end of this unit, students will:
- understand the purpose of a reference list and bibliography
- be able to produce a reference list and bibliography using the APA system

Task 1 Reference list or bibliography?

1.1 Pairwork

Students follow instructions in the Student's Book.

Answers:
a. The purpose of a reference list is:
- to credit authors of the sources used in a piece of work
- to enable the reader to locate these sources

b. A *bibliography* includes all the sources used in preparation of a piece of work, whether cited in the text or not. A *reference list* only includes sources which are cited in a piece of work.

c. Journal articles often have a reference list, whereas books tend to have bibliographies. It is worth stressing to your students that they should always check which is required of them for any one particular assignment.

d. An author may choose to include a bibliography rather than a reference list in order to acknowledge all of the sources they used in their research, rather than only those they have cited.

e. Reference list. It is important to cite the sources of information and graphics used in a presentation on the slides where the content appears. The full information about each source used should be in a reference list in APA format at the end.

Task 2 The APA style for referencing

Elicit from students examples of referencing systems which are frequently used in their particular disciplines. Explain that APA is one of many referencing systems, and that the main focus of the subsequent tasks is not so much to learn how to use APA as to practise accurate use of one referencing system.

Discuss with students the need for them to find out which referencing system should be used in any one module. Elicit where they would look for this type of information (departmental website, student handbook, module handbook, assignment instructions, etc.).

2.1 Individual work/Pairwork

Focus students' attention on the example of a book reference and elicit what the various components mean, e.g., What does *2012* refer to? Then ask students to work individually writing the jumbled-up components in *Task 2.1* in the correct order, and then compare their answer with a partner's. When you are checking the answer with the class, ask which component or components should be written in italics.

Answer:
Oatley, T. H. (2012). *International political economy* (5th ed.). London, England: Longman.

Note: *The location of a publisher within the US is given as the city and state. For publishers outside the US, the city and country should be given for the location.*

2.2 Pairwork

In pairs, students answer the questions.

Answers:
a.
- Additional information is added, including the chapter title and the name of the editor, which comes after the year of publication and before the title of the book.
- The chapter title is not in italics.
- The initials of the editor come before the surname.
- The page numbers of the chapter are inserted after the book title.

b.
- *Ed.* stands for editor.

2.3 Pairwork

In pairs, students answer the questions.

Answers:
a. Probing the NASPH-binding site of escherichia coli flavodoxin oxidoreductase

b. 7. Where the reference in the Student's Book includes an ellipsis in the list of authors. However, it should be noted that the ellipsis (…) between the penultimate and final author's name indicates that the article has a large number of authors, and so some of their names have been omitted for reasons of space. In this particular example, the original article has 11 authors:
Leadbeater, C., McIver, L., Campopiano, C. J., Webster, S. P., Baxter, R. L., Kelly S. M., (…) Wunro, A. W. (2000). Probing the NASPH-binding site of escherichia coli flavodoxin oxidoreductase. *Biochemical Journal, 352*, 257-266.

c. *Biochemical Journal*

d. Journals are subdivided into volumes. In the example, *352* is the volume number of the journal.

e. *257–266* refers to the page range of the article.

2.4 Individual work

This task could be set for homework as it offers students the opportunity to practise their citation skills in relation to their (future) discipline. Students should write citations for three hard copy sources of the periodical type.

Answers:
Answers will vary from student to student.

2.5 Individual work

Students follow instructions in the Student's Book.

Answer:
Banks, N., Hulme, D., & Edwards, M. (2014). NGOs, states, and donors revisited: Still too close for comfort? *World Development, 66*, 707–718.

Task 3 Referencing sources accessed online

3.1 Individual work

Focus students' attention on the example format. Elicit what XXX–XXX refers to (page range of article). Students then follow instructions in the Student's Book.

Answer:

Belton, B., & Thilsted, S.H. (2014). Fisheries in transition: Food and nutrition security implications for the global South. *Global Food Security, 3*(1), 59–66. http://dx.doi.org/10.1016/j.gfs.2013.10.001

3.2 Individual work

If students are finding referencing sources accessed online challenging, you may want to spend some time going through the introduction to the task before setting it.

Answers:

a. Conversi (2010) was retrieved from the journal website, and Copland (2012) was retrieved from an alternative website. The last part of the URL gives this information.

b. It is preferred to include the DOI, rather than the URL, in a reference where a DOI exists, because the site hosting an article may change and so the URL may no longer lead to the article. In contrast, the DOI provides a permanent link to the article.

c. Magazines are periodicals, as are journals, and so often have volume and issue numbers. They are less likely to use DOIs, so where a DOI is not given, the URL should be used.

3.3 Individual work

Students follow instructions in the Student's Book.

Answers:

Similarities

- The homepage link is given rather than the article link. This is done so that you can search for the article from the homepage, and so that you can avoid the potential problem of nonworking URLs.
- The newspaper name is in italics, similar to a journal title. Other formatting is the same.

Differences

- The date of publication is included in the parentheses with the year. This is because newspapers are documented according to date of publication and so too are newspaper articles published online.

Task 4 Referencing articles on websites

Many university library websites publish material on identifying reliable sources. If appropriate, make your students aware of where they can access such information in their own (future) institutions.

4.1 Pairwork

Ask students to read the introduction to the task. If appropriate, clarify the meaning of a **stand-alone report**. Students then discuss the questions in pairs.

Answers:

a. The website URL for Harrison (2011) contains the abbreviation *bbc*, which stands for British Broadcasting Corporation. While the abbreviation BBC may be well known in the UK, it may be less well known outside of the UK. Forbes is clearly stated in the URL for Smith (2013).

b. The document written by Johnson (2012) is a stand-alone report and so is put in italics. Generally titles of webpages, articles, blog post, messages and news items on webpages are not put italics.

4.2 Pairwork

Students follow instructions in the Student's Book.

Answers:

a. As blog entries are frequently published, a date of publication is included.

b. The organisation name is not included in the retrieval information as the APA has already been given as the group author name.

c. In the third example listed, the BBC is not given as a corporate author because the reference is to a news item appearing on a website. The item is not a policy or report published by a group author; rather, it is an article from which the author's name has been omitted. In this type of case, the title of the article is given at the beginning of the reference.

d. When no author is named, the title of the article appears first, followed by the year in parenthesis, and then the retrieval information which gives the URL. An in-text citation for this source would be: "US economy contracted" (2014). In the reference list, due to the absence of an author's name, the first letters of the title would be used to place it in alphabetical order.

Task 5 Further resources

Again, many university library websites give links to information on how to reference a wide range of source types. If appropriate, make your students aware of where they can access such information in their (future) institution.

5.1 Classwork

Discuss as a class.

Answers:

After the title, the type of source is stated when the information has come from a more unusual type, for example, a blog or a PDF. Information on the type of source is put in square parentheses followed by a full-stop.

3 The mechanics of citations

At the end of this unit, students will be able to:
*   use direct and indirect quotations or citations in their writing
*   understand the differences between paraphrasing and summarising

Task 1 When to use citations

1.1 Pairwork

Students follow instructions in the Student's Book.

Answers:
a.   reference
b.   reference
c.   not reference – with the proviso that the idea does not also exist in the literature
d.   reference
e.   reference
f.   not reference
g.   reference

1.2 Pairwork

Ask students to read the excerpt from an essay and infer the topic of the essay. Then ask students to re-read the excerpt, paying attention to the use of a direct quotation.

Answers:
a.   The essay writer quotes Szasz because Szasz's use of parallel clause structures makes the idea clearly and memorably.
b.   The words within quotation marks are taken from Szasz's book.
c.   Szasz is the author's family name.
d.   The essay writer doesn't include initials in the text as these are not necessary to identify the source.
e.   The essay writer's words are all those which don't appear within quotation marks.
f.   The essay writer included *1974* in brackets to signal the year of publication.
g.   *p.124* refers to the page of Szasz's book where the quotation can be found. The essay writer included the information so that the reader can read the quote in its original context.

Task 2 Reasons for using direct quotations

2.1 Individual work/Pairwork

Ask students to work individually, and then compare their answers in pairs.

Answers:
a.   vivid
b.   summarised
c.   misrepresentation
d.   easier

Task 3 Longer direct quotations: block style

3.1 Pairwork

Ask students to read the introduction and example, and then compare these with the example of a short quotation in *Task 1.2* of this unit. Students then work in pairs to discuss the questions.

Answers:
a.   The quotation is indented.
b.   The writer used three dots to show one or more words have been omitted.
c.   The page number immediately follows the direct quotation.
d.   There is no definite maximum length for a quotation, but many authorities suggest somewhere between six or eight lines of text.
e.   It isn't considered good style to have too many block quotations in an essay as it may distract the reader from your argument, or make the style of your writing seem choppy.

Task 4 Choosing what to quote directly

Ask students for examples of direct quotations from their disciplines as a lead-in to the task.

4.1 Pairwork

Ask students to work in pairs, deciding which of the quotations they would keep as direct quotations in a piece of work, giving reasons for their decisions.

Answers:
a and c

Elicit what the quotations of Einstein and Confucius have in common which make them appropriate for direct quotation – their vivid and memorable form.

Task 5 Indirect quotations or citations

5.1 & 5.2 Pairwork

Ask students to read the introduction to the task, and then compare the example of an indirect quotation of Attenborough (1984) with the original text on page 19 of the Student's Book.

Answers:
5.1
This is a summary as Attenborough's ideas have been compressed, rather than rephrased.
5.2
a.   We can tackle global warming by reducing waste, which includes unnecessary travel (Attenborough, 1984).
b.   Attenborough (1984) argues that we can tackle global warming by reducing waste, which includes unnecessary travel.
c.   In a recent article, Attenborough (1984) argues that we can tackle global warming by reducing waste, which includes unnecessary travel.

You may wish to ask students what they should consider when choosing which form to use, e.g., in sentence a, the essay writer's voice is much 'louder' than Attenborough's. This is not the case for sentence b, where Attenborough is the subject of the reporting verb.

Note: *Some universities or university departments require page numbers to be given for indirect quotations where these refer to a particular part of a text. Students should check what is required of them.*

Task 6 Reporting verbs

In order to introduce the topic of reporting verbs, you could focus students' attention on the wordle in the Student's Book and ask them which ones are most common in their disciplines.

6.1 Pairwork

Students follow instructions in the Student's Book.

Answers:
a. 4
b. 3
c. 1
d. 5
e. 2

In order to help students develop their sense of an author's stance, you could ask them to examine reporting verbs in a text taken from their discipline, noting how the verbs contribute to the author's argument.

Task 7 Practice using indirect quotations

7.1 Individual work

Depending on the ability of your students, you may wish to spend time working on the meaning of the original text before students close their books and write a summary of the text. In the correction phase of the task, ask students to justify their selection of reporting verb.

Answers:
Answers will vary from student to student.

7.2 Classwork/Small group work

Ask students to work in small groups, comparing their indirect quotations and selecting the best. Then compare each group's indirect quotation as a class. Ask students to create a checklist they can use to evaluate their indirect quotations in the future, e.g.:
• Don't change the meaning of the original.
• Don't add my own ideas to the original idea.

 4 Reading and note-taking

At the end of this unit, students will be able to:
• take effective notes to avoid plagiarism
• paraphrase and summarise naturally

Task 1 Reading and note-taking

1.1 Individual work/Pairwork

With Student's Books closed, write the essay title given on page 23 of the Student's Book on the board and ask pairs of students to brainstorm a set of reading questions in relation to the title. Then ask students to compare their reading questions with those in the Student's Book.

Before asking students to work alone taking notes, you may wish to revise the characteristics of effective notes. Ask students to complete the note-taking task, and then assess their notes using the characteristics to aid them.

Answers:
a. Overall, it is difficult to say whether English is easy to learn. Learning to write English may be easier than learning to write Chinese or Arabic. In terms of mastering the sound system, English would be in the middle of a scale from most to least complex.
b. The answer to this question depends on which aspect of a language is being focused on.
c. Yes
d. Yes

1.2 Individual work

Ask students to write a paragraph of their choice. These could then form the basis of a wall-display.

Answers:
Answers will vary from student to student.

5 Using sources effectively

At the end of this unit, students will be able to:
*   put into practice what they have learned

Task 1 Acceptable use of external sources of information (books, journals, internet sites)

1.1 Small group work

Students follow instructions in the Student's Book. Ask students to give reasons for their answers.

Answers:
a and e are acceptable

Task 2 Who has got it right?

2.1 Small group work

Students follow instructions in the Student's Book. They should be able to justify their answers.

Answers:
a.   Incorrect use of source – no acknowledgement made of the source.
b.   Incorrect use of source – contains verbatim uses of the source's language without showing this with quotation marks.
c.   Correct

Module 8 Presentations

1 About presentations

At the end of this unit, students will:
- recognise what makes a good presentation
- understand the process of preparing a presentation

Task 1 What makes a good presentation

Lead in by focusing students' attention on the visual and eliciting whether the presentation is formal or informal, academic or non-academic.

1.1 Small group work

Students should draw on their own experiences. Your role is to facilitate discussion.

Encourage the groups to make notes.

Possible answers:
a. Interesting topic for the audience, evidence of thorough research, good organisation, explanation of technical terms, clear presentation, good use of eye contact and body language, interesting visuals, use of appropriate vocabulary and grammar.
b. Boring topic for the audience, inappropriate content for audience, disorganised, voice too quiet/loud, not enough eye contact, speaking speed too fast or too slow, flat intonation, language inaccuracy, lack of acknowledgement of sources used.

1.2 Pairwork

This activity will provide you with useful information on your students' current presentation skills, e.g., selection and organisation of information, use of notes, delivery style, etc.

Students should be divided into A/B pairs, allotted a task and given a few minutes to prepare a brief presentation of 1–2 minutes. Students should take notes on their partner's presentation to use in a later activity. Do not discuss the answers to the questions at this point.

1.3 Pairwork

Students follow instructions in the Student's Book. Ask students to make a note of their priorities for improvement in a presentation diary they keep during the module.

Task 2 Planning checklist

2.1 Pairwork

Students follow instructions in the Student's Book. As they work through the task, encourage students to think about why their answers to *Task 1.2* may have differed. On completion, discuss any queries as a class.

Task 3 Grading criteria

3.1 Pairwork

Lead in by asking your class to recall what aspects or criteria their teachers have used to mark their presentations in the past. Elicit whether students used these criteria to plan their previous presentation(s).

If students get stuck, direct their attention to the visual in *Task 3.1* and the planning checklist in *Task 2*.

Possible answers:
Content: appropriate material – amount, level
Delivery: clear explanations of technical terms, clear pronunciation
Organisation: well-planned, clear structure, logical sequence
Visual aids: used to support message academic requirements: appropriate register, acknowledgement of sources
Response to questions: clear, concise, further examples
Teamwork: material well divided between group, evidence of group practice
Research: evidence of research, appropriate choice of sources
Argumentation: clear research focus, good selection of ideas and evidence
Language accuracy: appropriate vocabulary and structure

2 Group presentations

At the end of this unit, students will:
- understand how to organise the preparation process
- understand how to share roles and responsibilities

The outcome of *Module 8* is a group presentation. As *Unit 2* introduces the notion of a group presentation, allocate students to presentation groups during this lesson. Each group should select a topic, possibly around a collective theme, brainstorm ideas, find a focus and then agree a research question before the end of the lesson. The group should then carry out an initial research phase before moving on to *Unit 3*. You might like to ask your students to detail the steps they took to prepare for the presentation, along with their responses to the reflection questions set at the end of each unit in their presentation diaries.

Your students may be interested in identifying their strengths and weaknesses as team members. The Belbin analysis of team roles may provide a useful starting point: http://www.belbin.com/rte.asp?id=8.

Task 1 Advantages and disadvantages

1.1 Small group work

Students follow instructions in the Student's Book.

Possible answers:
a.   **advantages**
  • You can learn from one another.
  • You can share ideas.
  • You can develop leadership and/or team-working skills.
b.   **disadvantages**
  • It can be time-consuming.
  • Some group members may make less effort or contribute less than others.
  • One or more group members may dominate.

Task 2 Working together

This and the remaining tasks in *Unit 2* require students to focus on time and people management skills. Remind your students to keep the outcomes of the activities in their presentation diaries, for example, *Tasks 2.1* and *3.1*.

The groups should be encouraged to keep a careful note of all sources used so that an accurate bibliography can be produced at a later date. It is usually best if one group member takes responsibility for this task.

2.1 & 2.2 Small group work

Students follow instructions in the Student's Book.

2.2

Answers:

team tasks	individual tasks
• set deadlines • select a team coordinator • discuss the distribution of research amongst group members • individuals share their findings with the rest of the team • plan who will do or say what	• set individual deadlines • conduct research on the presentation topic

Task 3 Group planning

3.1 Small group work

Students follow instructions in the Student's Book.

Possible answers:
One possible logical order:
1.   Record the names and contact information for all group members
2.   Arrange a preliminary meeting to agree how to proceed
3.   Schedule regular meetings in advance
4.   Set up a way to share documents (Dropbox, Google Docs, etc.)
5.   Discuss what the presentation assignment means
6.   Divide the presentation assignment into smaller tasks
7.   Share responsibilities equally
8.   Set deadlines for the completion of tasks
9.   Write meeting notes with action points
10.   Distribute meeting notes to other members
11.   Give each other feedback

Task 4 Group work

4.1 & 4.2 Pairwork/Small group work

Students follow instructions in the Student's Book, forming pairs within their presentation groups. At the end, ask students to feedback to the class about the criteria they found easy to apply and those they didn't.

Reflect

Ask students to add the table of responsibilities in the Reflect section of their presentation diaries.

3 Content

At the end of this unit, students will:
  • understand how to define their topic and purpose
  • be able to plan a presentation
  • be aware of appropriate presentation structure

Task 1 Defining your purpose

1.1, 1.2 & 1.3 Individual work/Group work

In this task, students are encouraged to identify the purpose of their presentation. To help students clarify the different purposes given in the Student's Book, it may be useful to give them examples of presentation titles and ask them to match them to the purposes given before setting *Task 1.1*.

Answers:
Answers will vary from group to group.

Task 2 Presentation structure

2.1 Individual work/Classwork

Students follow instructions in the Student's Book. Elicit the structure of a presentation from the class.

Possible answer:
Say what you are going to say, say it, say what you have said. It may be helpful to draw out the similarity with the macro-organisation of an essay.

2.2 Small group work/Classwork

Students follow instructions in the Student's Book. It may be necessary to emphasise that, at this stage, what is required is a **brief overview** of the presentation. Point out that it is a useful opportunity for the groups to find out what the future audience knows about the topic, what it is interested in, and how much technical language it is familiar with. This information could be recorded in their presentation diaries and used at a planning meeting.
To practise what was learned in *Task 1.1*, you could elicit the main purpose of each presentation from the other groups listening.

Task 3 Planning your presentation

3.1 Small group work
Students follow instructions in the Student's Book.

3.2 Small group work
Depending on the students, you may need to clarify the meaning of **detail**, **explanation** and **evidence**. One way of doing this would be to elicit examples from the class.

3.3 Small group work/Classwork
Ask students to read the introduction to the task and suggest some dos and don'ts for conclusions. Students then follow instructions in the Student's Book, presenting their conclusions to the class in order to evaluate how clearly they have communicated their 'take home' messages. They should make a note of how well they achieved this in their diaries.

The groups should then discuss which of the additional steps given in the Student's Book they wish to include. For information on preparing a bibliography, refer your students to *TASK Module 7: Referencing & Avoiding Plagiarism*.

3.4 Small group work
Students follow instructions in the Student's Book.

Task 4 Preparing notes

To preface this task, it may be useful to raise students' consciousness of the differences between spoken and written language, particularly if you think they may write a complete transcript of the presentation which draws heavily on the language of the written sources they are using. To do this, play them a 60-second clip from a lecture and then ask them to read the first few lines of a research article on the same topic. Elicit some of the key differences in language, e.g., sentence length, sentence complexity, use of repetition, etc.

4.1 Small group work
If your students find the idea of presenting from anything other than a full script daunting, it may be worth referring them back to *Unit 1, Task 1*, and eliciting what the dangers of reading aloud might be.

Answers:
See table below.

4.2 Individual/Small group work
Ask students to work individually at first, creating a set of notes. They subsequently compare their notes, discussing the pros and cons of their choices.

Possible answers (Task 4.1):

	advantages	disadvantages
Memorising your talk	• nothing is left to chance • the speaker can move around	• the presenter sounds bored • the presenter forgets • the presenter's intonation is flat • the presenter looks to the left because he/she is remembering • the language is more formal because it's written in complete sentences
Writing a list of bullet points on sheets of paper	• the key points are clear • easy to adapt to time constraints • the language is less likely to be too close to formal written form • the speaker can move around	• the paper may distract the audience – the presenter might obscure his/her face, or may shake it if nervous • paper can be dropped
Writing each key idea on a separate notecard	• easy to manage • the speaker can move around • the language is less likely to be too close to formal written form	• not always easy to know how many points are remaining when speaking • notecards can be dropped
Using the notes function within your presentation software	• restricted space makes the note-writer focus on the key message on the slide • easy to use • the language is less likely to be too close to formal written form	• not always easy to read due to glare • presenter may look at the screen rather than audience • if the speaker is moving the slides on and has no clicker, he/she cannot move around easily • if there are technical problems, the presenter has no access to the notes
Using the screen as a prompt (without additional notes)	• the speaker can move around • the language is less likely to be too close to formal written form	• the speaker simply reads the slides aloud • if there are technical problems, the presenter has no access to the notes

4 Visual aids

At the end of this unit, students will:
- be more familiar with a range of appropriate visual aids
- be able to design and use visual aids effectively

Task 1 Why use visual aids?

Show your class some infographics (e.g., http://www.informationisbeautiful.net/visualizations/) and elicit how they communicate information effectively, engage the audience and help an audience understand complex information.

1.1 Small group work

Presentation groups should discuss the question set and make notes.

Task 2 Choosing and using visual aids

2.1 Pairwork

Students follow instructions in the Student's Book, making notes in the table.

Answers:
See table below.

2.2 Pairwork

Focus students' attention on the graphic. Ask whether it is a good or bad example of a visual aid and then ask students to discuss why each don't in the list is a problem.

Answers:
DON'T:
- **crowd too much information into one visual**
  It can make it difficult to read.
- **stand in front of the visual aid**
  It can make it difficult to read.
- **read directly from the main screen or visual**
  It is boring for the audience.
- **put unimportant details in the visual**
  It's distracting.
- **forget to talk about information in a visual**
  It's confusing for the audience.
- **use a font that is too small**
  It can make it difficult to read.
- **put visuals in a different order to that of the information in the presentation**
  It will confuse the audience and is evidence of poor preparation.

2.3 Small group work

Focus students' attention on the graphic again, this time eliciting **why** it is a bad example of a visual.

Possible answers:
- Too many different types of information on one visual.
- Long chunks of text.
- Some text is in a font too small to read.
- Distracting and unnecessary photos cluttering the visual.
- Unexplained figures.

Task 3 Choosing what to write and what to say

3.1 Pairwork

Students follow instructions in the Student's Book.

Possible answers:
Problems of writing too much text without providing any visuals:
- key message gets lost
- audience is distracted
- presenter reads slide aloud

Problems of showing an image without explanation:
- key message gets lost
- audience is distracted

Possible answers (Task 2.1):

visual aid	advantages	disadvantages
posters	• a lot of information in one place	• time-consuming to prepare • difficult for the audience to read
presentation software (Microsoft PowerPoint®, Prezi)	• look professional	• time-consuming to prepare • technical problems may arise
videos	• visually appealing • contain a lot of information	• the presenter cannot speak at the same time
whiteboard	• no preparation required	• takes time during the presentation • the presenter has his/her back turned to the audience
printed handouts	• can provide a useful summary to take away	• audience may divide its attention between handout and speaker
props	• engaging for audience	• may distract audience, particularly if passed round

3.2 Small group work

Remind students of the importance of listening to all the group members' opinions, but also of coming to a consensus about the content to be included.

Possible answer:

Why study a foreign language?

Benefits include:

- Intercultural awareness
- Better employability
- Increased mobility
- Personal satisfaction

Task 4 Preparing posters

Lead in by showing some examples of presentation posters to the class. Elicit if anyone in the class has given or attended a poster presentation.

4.1 Classwork

With books closed, ask what the key differences are between posters and presentation software such as PowerPoint.

Possible answers:
- Presentation software allows the presenter to reveal information step-by-step, while this is not possible with a poster.
- Presentation software is dynamic, and may also include sound effects which, if used wisely, may be engaging for the audience.
- Posters can be used to create a good small-group focus.
- Posters are useful if you wish the audience to ask questions at the end of the presentation as all the information is on display.

4.2 Pairwork

With books closed, ask students to brainstorm questions that should be asked when preparing a visual aid. Ask students to check their ideas by reading through the example in *Task 4.2*.

4.3 Pairwork

Students follow instructions in the Student's Book. They can be encouraged to keep a record of their findings in their presentation diaries, along with their thoughts on the reflection questions.

Answers:
Answers will vary from student to student.

5 Delivery

At the end of this unit, students will:
- be more familiar with the language of presentations
- be able to use appropriate body language

Task 1 The language of presentations

1.1 & 1.2 Individual work/Pairwork

Lead in by eliciting the function of signposts on a road. Focus the group's attention on the phrases presented in *Task 1.1* and elicit how these function like a signpost, before setting the task.

If your students use English as an additional language, you may need to drill the pronunciation of the phrases. To give students further practice, divide them into pairs. Partners take it in turns to say a phrase which the other person paraphrases.

To give students further practice, refer them back to the choice of presentation topics in *Unit 2, Task 4*. Ask them to give a three-minute-presentation on one of the topics, using the phrases given to a partner, who ticks every phrase in *Tasks 1.1* and *1.2* they hear.

Answers:
1.1
a. 2
b. 4
c. 3
d. 5
e. 1
1.2
f. 6
g. 8
h. 9
i. 10
j. 7

Task 2 Using your voice effectively

2.1 & 2.2 Small group work

Students follow instructions in the Student's Book.

Possible answers:

Speed	Don't speak too quickly. Look at the audience to check that they can still follow you. It's also a mistake to speak too slowly.
Intonation	Vary the intonation of your voice to show emotion or meaning. When asking questions, for example, use appropriate intonation. Use intonation and tonic stress to emphasise key ideas.
Pauses	Use pauses around key ideas or words, or use them to give the audience time to follow your ideas.
Emphasis	Emphasise key words to show that they are more important.

Task 3 Body language

3.1 Pairwork

Students follow instructions in the Student's Book.

Possible answers:
smile at the audience:
seems welcoming, confident and friendly, and builds trust
sit down:
could make the speaker seem uninterested and make him/her harder to hear
walk around:
this could be distracting; however, measured movement can look purposeful
look only at notes:
makes it hard to hear the speaker, and will make his/her delivery less interesting
use hand gestures:
can create interest and add emphasis
make eye contact with audience:
engages and holds the audience's attention
play with hair/change in pocket/earring, etc.:
can be distracting
lean against a wall:
can make the speaker seem uninterested
point at the audience:
might seem aggressive

3.2 Small group work

Students follow instructions in the Student's Book. Students could be asked to write up their discussions on one or both questions in their presentation diaries.

Answers:
Answers will vary from group to group.

Task 4 Rehearsing your presentation

4.1 Small group work

As a lead-in, ask why rehearsing a presentation together is important, and then ask students to read the introduction to the task to check their answers. Also point out the importance of handing over smoothly from speaker to speaker within the group and of group members dressing with roughly the same level of formality.

After groups have given their presentations, ask them to review the notes they have made in their presentation diary in order to reflect on:
*   areas of progress
*   areas which require further work
*   the highs and lows of giving a group presentation

Understanding assessment tasks

At the end of this unit, students will:
- understand how to answer essay questions
- be able to maximise their performance on multiple-choice questions

Task 1 Instruction words

Before the class, it may be useful for you or your students to find examples of past papers in their discipline.

1.1 Individual work

Alternatively, you could copy each keyword and explanation onto a small card and use these in a vocabulary snowball activity. For this, give each student a card and ask him/her to read it, check any unknown vocabulary in a dictionary, and then learn the keyword and definition. Students should then move around the classroom, teaching their word to a classmate, who reciprocates. When both students have finished explaining their word, the pair swaps cards. Each student then looks for a new classmate to teach his/her new keyword and explanation to, swapping cards again, and so on until the whole group has learned all of the words. At the end of the activity, ask students to complete *Task 1.1* on page 2 of the Student's Book.

Answers:

a. comment on: Identify the main issues and give an informed opinion.

contrast: Show how two things are different. Explain the consequences of dissimilarities.

analyse: Examine in detail by dividing up. Identify the main points.

define: Give the precise meaning of a term. This may include explaining what is problematic about defining the term.

compare: Show how two things are similar. Explain the consequences of the similarities.

b. discuss: Look at the most important aspects of something in a balanced way, i.e., advantages and disadvantages, for and against.

describe: Give the main features, characteristics or events.

evaluate: Assess how important or useful something is. It is likely to include both positive and negative points.

explain: Provide reasons for why something happens, or why something is in a particular state.

examine: Take a detailed look at something.

c. make a case: Put forward an argument either for or against a claim.

interpret: Give the meaning or significance of something.

outline: Give the main ideas or information, without any details.

illustrate: Show what something is like, using examples and/or evidence.

justify: Support a claim with evidence, taking into account opposing views.

d. trace: Put the steps and stages of a process or event into order.

summarise: Give the main points only, using fewer words than the original.

relate: Give the connections between things.

to what extent: Say how much something is or isn't true.

state: Give just the main points, very clearly.

1.2 Pairwork/Classwork

Ask students to compare their answers in pairs, and then discuss as a class. Put some questions on the board, omitting the instruction word, and elicit which words might complete the questions.

1.3 Pairwork/Classwork

Lead in by asking students to identify the political event being alluded to in the visual. Ask students to discuss how the change in instruction words results in a change in the task. You could allot each pair an essay title and ask them to discuss what the main sections of their essay would be; then compare ideas as a whole class.

Answers:

a. *Trace* would generally imply a description from one point to another.

b. *Interpret* would generally expect students to analyse and evaluate. The word **significance** in this case also highlights the need for evaluation.

c. *Analyse* would require students to look in detail at the issue.

1.4 Pairwork

Students follow instructions in the Student's Book

Answers:
Answers will vary from student to student.

Task 2 Question styles

2.1 Pairwork/Small group work

This task is particularly applicable when students are required to transfer these skills to other disciplines. Set up the task as pairwork, and then elicit ideas for each question. If students are studying a range of disciplines, you could also compare and contrast the different approaches. If your students have access to past papers, ask them to refer to the papers during this task.

Task 3 Exam essay planning and title analysis

3.1 Individual work/Pairwork

Lead in by asking students if they know (of) anyone who speaks and writes English very fluently and accurately without ever having lived in an English-speaking country. Students work individually, and then compare their answers with a partner's.

Answers:
a. 2
b. Is living in an English-speaking country the best way to learn English?
c. Is it impossible to learn English without living in an English-speaking environment?
d. 3 – Look at the question in a balanced way.

3.2 Individual work/Pairwork

Ask students to plan their answer to the question, and then compare their plans with a partner's. Finally, ask students to compare their plan with the one on page 29 of the Student's Book.

Answers:
Part 1
*   Is studying the English language in an English-speaking country the best way to learn the language?
*   Are there any other ways of learning a language effectively?
Part 2
*   Is it true that it is not possible to learn the English language without spending time living in an Anglophone environment?
Essay plan
*   Introduction, including definition of key terms and a thesis statement. (Use James and Miller quote.)
*   Explain the advantages of studying in the home culture in order to learn basic grammar. (Use cautious language, e.g., One advantage may be …)
*   (Signposting, e.g., On the other hand, …) Describe the advantages of studying in an Anglophone environment in order to practise listening and speaking. (Use cautious language.)
*   (Signposting, e.g., To conclude …) Conclude that learning the basic grammar may be more effective in the home culture and that developing listening and speaking skills is often more successful in an English-speaking country.

Task 4 Planning and analysis in practice

4.1 Individual work/Pairwork

Encourage your students to think about how many parts the essay has, what issues should be covered and the nature of the overall task. Refer them to *TASK Module 4: Essay Writing* for further help.

Alternatively, this task could be set for homework and the plans produced by your students could form the basis of either a tutorial or a peer evaluation of the plan session.

Answers:
a. There are two parts:
    Part 1:   Secondary schools should redesign the curriculum in order to concentrate solely on teaching children the academic disciplines that are required for employment.
    Part 2:   It is a waste of time to devote school-time to subjects such as Arts and General Studies.
    The essay is asking students to argue which of the two stances taken is the better one.
b. There are two parts, but one is not obviously stated:
    Part 1:   Examinations are the best way to judge student performance.
    Part 2:   Other methods are ineffective.
    The essay is asking students to judge the effectiveness of examinations as an assessment tool.

Task 5 Identifying examinations skills

5.1 & 5.2 Pairwork

Ask students to work with a partner to brainstorm the type of questions they might need to answer in an exam. Ask students to think about the possible skills they might need for each one. Point out that some skills might be similar.

Answers:

type of question	skills practice required
Answering questions based on a text	• understanding questions fully • skimming and scanning
Essay writing	• essay planning • title analysis
Multiple choice	• demonstrate basic knowledge of a subject. distinguish between similar answers
Short answers	• writing definitions
Report writing	• planning, structure and clarity
Problem solving, e.g., mathematical questions	• logic; use of mathematical formula
Data analysis	• analysis and interpretation of the significance of the data

Task 6 Timed essay writing

6.1 Individual work

This task could be set for homework.

Task 7 Answering multiple-choice questions

7.1 Individual work

Ask students to read the text and practise this technique on some multiple-choice English language questions before trying the technique out on a past exam paper relevant to their academic discipline(s).

Task 8 Short answer questions

8.1 Individual work

Explain to students that many short answer questions often require students to write definitions or explanations of key terms. Ask students to match the functions to the sentences in the short answer.

Answers:
a. 3
b. 4
c. 2
d. 1

8.2 Individual work

Set this task for homework. In a following class, ask students to identify the features from the model in their partner's paragraph.

If you are aiming to teach *Unit 2* next, ask your students to bring along a set of notes on a topic related to their subject.

2 Study skills and active learning

At the end of this unit, students will:
*   understand various study skills strategies
*   use strategies to help them to memorise information

Task 1 Study skills

This task encourages students to think about and evaluate their own study skills.

1.1 & 1.2 Pairwork/Small group work

Ask students to read the headings of the three sections and to predict what they think each section will be about. Check students' predictions.

Ask students to put the techniques in order from the most effective to the least effective, to compare their order in groups, and then to elicit an order with reasons.

Answers:
Students can put forward a case for any order. Research by Dunlosky et al. (2012) would suggest the order is: Practice testing, Self-explanation and Highlighting.

1.3 Pairwork

Set the task as an individual reading task first and then ask students to discuss their answers with a partner.

Answers:
a. It doesn't require any training and makes students feel like they are busy.
b. According to Dunlosky et al. (2012) the technique is not very effective for learning for a test, but it is effective for understanding a theory. It isn't good for developing deep knowledge as it doesn't require students to question or challenge ideas.
c. Practice testing gets students familiar with test formats. It also highlights weaknesses in knowledge. Distributed practice is better for consolidating knowledge than cramming as it builds knowledge gradually.

1.4 & 1.5 Pairwork

Set the task as an individual reading task first and then ask students to discuss their answers with a partner.

Answers:
1.4
a. interleaved practice
b. elaborative interrogation
1.5
a. Answers will vary from student to student.
b. Both techniques have been shown to aid understanding and recall possibly because they require the person revising to be an active user of information and ideas, applying them to disciplinary problems.
c. Answers will vary from student to student.

Task 2 A deeper understanding

Ideally, students need a set of notes on a topic in their subject area for this task. Ask them to bring some along to the class, particularly if you decide not to do the extension activity suggested in *Task 2.2*.

Ask students to read the introduction to the task and elicit examples of core concepts.

2.1 Individual work

Students follow instructions in the Student's Book. Alternatively, you could bring a picture of an object cut into pieces and give students one piece each, telling them to keep it hidden. Ask them to take it in turns to describe their piece and elicit the name of the object. Then ask the group to fit the pieces of the puzzle together to check if their proposed answers were correct.

At the end of the task, elicit examples of core concepts and their parts.

2.2 Individual work/Pairwork

Students follow instructions in the Student's Book. You could extend this activity by finding a description of a core concept in your students' area of study, if they are following the same or a similar discipline. Then ask students to identify the concept and its constituent parts and make notes in a table similar to the one in the task. If your class is mixed in terms of subject of study, you could have a research lesson in which you ask students to identify a core concept, find a relevant description and carry out the note-taking activity. In this case, you will need to support your students during the research activity as they might find it difficult to identify relevant material. If your students have access to a reading list for their future programme, they should be encouraged to use material indicated on this list.

Answers:

concept	parts
society	group of people
	particular place
	share a distinctive culture and set of institutions

Task 3 Organising information into groups

3.1, 3.2 & 3.3 Individual work/Pairwork

Set the first two memory tasks as individual tasks, and the third task as pairwork. In feedback stage, you might want to ask students how they learn vocabulary that they have, for example, encountered in a reading text.

Task 4 Reorganising information into diagrams

4.1 Individual work/Pairwork

Students follow instructions in the Student's Book. Having corrected the task, ask students if they already use any of the methods.

Answers:
a.   2
b.   3
c.   1

4.2 Individual work/Pairwork

The rewriting activity could be set for homework. If you used the extension activity suggested in *Task 2.2* of this unit – you could ask students to work with these notes.

In the discussion activity, encourage students to explain their choice of diagram as well as explaining the information contained in the diagram. Encourage students to reflect on which form(s) of diagrammatic note-taking best suit(s) the requirements of their own academic discipline.

Task 5 Reorganising information into summary notes

5.1 & 5.2 Individual work/Pairwork

As a lead-in to this task, it might be worth pointing out to your students that note-taking from previous scholarship and the use of these notes to write a summary is a very common academic routine. Encourage your group to make a note of the bibliographical details of their source text and to include these in their summary in an acceptable manner (see *TASK Module 7: Referencing & Avoiding Plagiarism* for more information).

In a class discussion at the end of the unit, in which you elicit from the group the main points they have learned, it may be worth drawing students' attention to the fact that teaching another person something is often an extremely good way of checking that you have a good grasp of the subject yourself. This is one reason why they should think about setting up a small study group when they start their academic programme.

If you are planning to teach *Unit 3* next, encourage your students to find an example of a past exam paper for one of the modules they will study on their future programme, and bring it to the lesson.

3 Planning for examinations

At the end of this unit, students will be able to:
- develop a good understanding of their examinations' requirements
- create a revision plan

Task 1 The purpose of examinations

This unit has been designed to meet the needs of students who are likely to sit an examination in the fairly near future. If this is the case, you could encourage your students to create a dedicated examination folder in which they collect relevant information about their examination(s). If, however, your students are not sitting an exam in the near future, you might prefer to look at *Task 1* and *Task 2.1* and then move on to *Unit 4*.

1.1 Pairwork

Students follow instructions in the Student's Book. Your role here is to facilitate discussion.

Answers:
Answers will vary from student to student.

1.2 Small group work

Students follow instructions in the Student's Book. Your role here is to facilitate discussion.

Answers:
a.
1. Examinations are a means by which lecturers can check students' understanding.
2. They are a way of encouraging intensive learning.

b.
1. The exam period is intense, and so study pressure is short-lived.
2. Exams encourage students to develop a good 'map' or overview of a subject.
3. There is less need for perfect presentation of written work.

Task 2 Examination requirements

If you think your students will struggle with this, it may be useful to have examples of some of the documents mentioned below. You could display the items, or printouts of them, on the classroom wall and ask students to match the descriptions of the documents listed with the realia. Alternatively, show students how to access electronic versions of the information where appropriate.

2.1 Pairwork

Students follow instructions in the Student's Book.

Possible answers:
a. student handbook
b. departmental/school website
c. learning outcomes of each module
d. lecture notes/lecture slides provided by lecturers
e. past exam papers
f. reading lists
g. comments on coursework

2.2 & 2.3 Individual work/pairwork

You may need to model this task for your students, showing how to synthesise information from a range of information sources.

Task 2.2 could be set for homework, particularly if you ask students to create a special examination folder in which they place:
- copies of the relevant documentation (see *Task 2.1*)
- a copy of the table giving key information about their examination(s) (see *Task 2.2*)

Task 2.3 is appropriate where you have two or more students sitting an examination in the same module/subject.

Task 3 Planning for an exam

3.1 Individual work/Pairwork/Classwork

Students need to organise this activity with subject tutors where possible.

Answers:
Answers will vary from student to student.

Task 4 Revision timetable

4.1 Individual work

This task could be set for homework and then form part of your students' examination folders.

Task 5 Revision timetable

As a lead-in, ask students to complete the following idiom: All work and no play … (makes Jack a dull boy). Elicit what the saying means and how it relates to revision planning.

5.1 Individual work

Elicit from the class the types of activities shown in the photos. Ask them which of the four would help them to relax best when under pressure. Then ask students to add some relaxation activities to their revision timetables. Alternatively, this task could be set for homework.

Reflect

Encourage students to add their thoughts on these questions to their examination folders.

 4 Revision strategies

At the end of this unit, students will:
- be aware of the benefits of active revision
- have a personal revision strategies toolkit

Task 1 Pass or fail

1.1 Individual work/Small group work

Students follow instructions in the Student's Book.

Possible answers:

pass	fail
• advance planning • good revision strategies • precise notes • extensive reading	• poor organisation • stress • lack of revision • illness

1.2 Pairwork

Students follow instructions in the Student's Book.

Answers:
Answers will vary from student to student.

Task 2 Active and passive revision

Lead in by eliciting from your students possible sources of advice available at university for students who are having problems with revising for an exam.

2.1 Individual work/Small group work

Ask your class to read the letter, underlining Olena's problems and possibly comparing their ideas with their partners', before they take notes.

2.2 Small group work

Encourage students to justify the advice they would give Olena.

2.3 Individual work/Pairwork

Depending on the preferences of your students, they could write individually or in pairs. This task could be set for homework.

As an alternative, you could ask pairs of students to prepare to role-play Olena's discussions with an academic adviser at her university.

Possible answers:
The reply should include some of the following points:
- spending time in a library is not the key solution to exam success
- break times should be more evenly divided throughout the day
- research suggests that it is impossible to concentrate for three hours at a time
- more breaks are recommended towards the end of the day, but breaks every 15 minutes may be disruptive
- you need a more evenly distributed timetable of revision
- choose a location without distractions
- reading without note-taking will not help to consolidate knowledge
- any problems with understanding the textbook should have been dealt with at an earlier stage

In order to encourage your students to develop their evaluation skills, you could make a wall display of all the replies to Olena's letter. Explain that the student newspaper can only publish one reply and that they, as members of the editorial board, have to make the decision about the best answer. Ask students to work in small groups and encourage them to develop a set of criteria for making their decision before they evaluate the letters. It would be useful to have a class session on these criteria before moving on to the evaluation stage. Alternatively, this evaluation stage could be carried out through a pyramid discussion.

Task 3 Reading past papers

3.1 Pairwork

Students follow instructions in the Student's Book.

Possible answers:
- To develop a better understanding of the paper.
- To find out how long the paper is.
- To work out how many questions you will have to answer.
- To note the sort of topics that appear regularly.
- To reduce the likelihood of an unpleasant surprise on the day of the exam.

3.2 Individual work

Stages 1–3 could be done in class, with Stage 4 set for homework.

Task 4 Revision toolkit

4.1 & 4.2 Individual work

These tasks could be set for homework and a copy of the list put in their examination folders. Encourage students to add further strategies, maybe garnered through talking to other students or through internet research.

Reflect

This activity also lends itself to an activity which could be included in their examination folders.

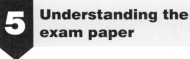

5 Understanding the exam paper

At the end of this unit, students will:
- understand how the question paper is organised
- be able to follow instructions on question papers more accurately

Task 1 The question paper cover

The activities in this unit could be applied to past exam papers supplied either by yourself or your students. If your students use English as an additional language, you may need to pre-teach the word **invigilator**.

1.1 Classwork

Use the following questions to check how much information students have identified from the exam cover:

- Is there an answer book?
- Where should the answers be written?
- What equipment is permitted?
- How long does the exam last?
- How much time is allowed for each section?
- How many marks are there for each section?
- What percentage of marks does each section contribute to the final total?
- Should students use some of the time to complete the front of the answer books?
- Why is a candidate number used rather than the candidate's name?

Answers:

- **Is there an answer book?** Yes
- **Where should the answers be written?** In the answer book.
- **What equipment is permitted?** A writing implement.
- **How long does the exam last?** 2 hours and 30 minutes
- **How much time is allowed for each section?** Listening, Reading & Grammar – 30 minutes each. Writing – 1 hour
- **How many marks are there for each section?** Listening, Reading & Grammar – 20 marks each. Writing – 40 marks
- **What percentage of marks does each section contribute to the final total?** 25%
- **Should students use some of the time to complete the front of the answer books?** No – extra time will be given for this at the end.
- **Why is a candidate number used rather than the candidate's name?** To reduce the likelihood of bias on the part of the marker.

Task 2 The rubric

2.1 Individual work/Pairwork

Explain to students that the most important factor in completing the exam efficiently is understanding the exam rubric completely and following the instructions exactly.

Answers:

- a. 1. The total number of questions that should be attempted.
  2. Instructions regarding which questions can be selected.
- b. 1. Answering the wrong number of questions or parts of questions, e.g., all the questions on the paper.
  2. Not following the instructions regarding the rules for selecting questions, e.g., choosing all questions from Section A.

Task 3 Following instructions

3.1 Individual work

In your lesson planning, be prepared for students either to work through this activity quickly or to spend as long as 15 minutes on it. Elicit what the take home message of the task is – to read the exam rubric carefully and to follow instructions.

3.2 Individual work/Pairwork

When introducing this activity, it is important to stress to the group that the activity is designed to test students' ability to follow instructions, not to test their knowledge of biology.

Answers:
Section A:
- students are only supposed to answer one of the three questions
- none of the questions are answered as instructed in the rubrics
Section B:
- only supposed to put one word in each space
- supposed to answer all parts
Section C:
- supposed to use chemical symbols for 7–9
- supposed to write the full name in 10

Reflect

Encourage students to do the task for homework and to add a record of this work in their examination folders.

6 Managing exam stress

At the end of this unit, students will be able to:

- understand how to manage anxiety while they are revising
- create a plan for managing their stress on the day of the exam

Task 1 Begin to take control

1.1 Pairwork

Lead in by eliciting what the visuals all have in common. Ask your students if they suffer from exam nerves and, if they do, how they cope with them. Then ask the pairs to review the work they have done in this module so far, selecting any ideas that would help them take control.

Task 2 Taking a positive attitude

2.1 & 2.2 Individual work/Pairwork

Students follow instructions in the Student's Book. Encourage pairs to discuss their previous experience of sitting exams when they do this evaluation task.

Answers:

- a. Deal with any pent-up energy by doing an energetic activity, e.g., jogging, dancing, and swimming.
- b. Revise with another student so that the process is not so lonely.
- c. Try to stay healthy by eating and sleeping well.

Task 3 Managing your anxiety

3.1 Individual work

Encourage students to underline keywords in the heading and in the brief descriptions of techniques in order to complete this task as rapidly as possible.

Answers:
a.   4
b.   5
c.   2
d.   3
e.   1

Task 4 Action points

4.1 Individual work

The work produced could be used to form a wall display. You could also ask your students to write down their own most important action points and keep this list in the front of their examination folders.

Reflect

Focus students on the reflection task, ask them to identify an example in their lives when stress brought about a positive outcome and add this example to their examination folders.

If your students have created examination folders while completing this module, encourage them to write a short reflection on how they have altered their attitudes to examinations and their examination preparation.

Module 10 Numeracy

1 Working with numbers

At the end of this unit, students will:
- learn how to work with fractions
- understand the meaning of percentages
- be able to use decimal numbers in calculations

Task 1 Simplifying fractions

1.1 Individual work/Pairwork

Ask students to complete the task individually, writing out their workings, and then compare their work with a partner's. Draw their attention to the fact that different workings can produce a correct answer.

If your students use English as an additional language, it may be useful to revise the vocabulary of fractions, e.g.:
a half
a third/two-thirds
a quarter/three-quarters
fifths/sixths/sevenths, etc.
Given that there is a fair amount of technical language connected with statistics, it may be worthwhile asking students to keep a vocabulary list of this for use at a later point in their studies.

Answers:
a. $\frac{60}{100}$ is $\frac{3}{5}$ in its smallest form.
b. $\frac{13}{22}$ is already in its smallest form and cannot be simplified.
c. $\frac{9}{81}$ is $\frac{1}{9}$ in its smallest form.

1.2 Individual work/Pairwork

Ask students to complete the task individually, writing out their workings, and then compare their work with a partner's. Again draw their attention to the fact that different workings can produce a correct answer.

Answer:
The correct answer is b) because $\frac{4}{9}$ is $\frac{64}{144}$ in its **simplest** form.

Task 2 Using fractions in practice

2.1 Individual work/Pairwork

Ask students to complete the task individually, writing out their workings, and then compare their answers with a partner's.

Answers:
a. Dividing 45 by 9 results in 5, then multiplying 5 by 2 gives 10.
b. Dividing 120 by 5 results in 24, then multiplying 24 by 4 gives 96.

Task 3 Finding a percentage of a quantity

3.1 Individual work/Pairwork

Ask students to complete the task individually, writing out their workings, and then compare their answers with a partner's.

Answers:
a. 160 divided by 100 is 1.6 and multiplying 1.6 by 10 gives 16, so 10% of 160 is 16.
b. 160 divided by 100 is 1.6 and multiplying 1.6 by 55 gives 88, so 55% of 160 is 88.
c. 160 divided by 100 is 1.6 and multiplying 1.6 by 80 gives 128, so 80% of 160 is 128.

3.2 Pairwork/Small group work

Explain to students that they are now going to apply their percentage skills to a problem. Ask students to work in pairs, first analysing the problem and then calculating the numbers of passengers by group. Pairs then compare their answers with another pair's.

Answers:
200 divided by 100 is 2.
Men: multiplying 2 by 48 gives 96, so there are 96 men on the airliner.
Women: multiplying 2 by 33 gives 66, so there are 66 women on the airliner.
Children: multiplying 2 by 19 gives 38, so there are 38 children on the airliner.

Task 4 Percentage increase and decrease

4.1 Individual work/Pairwork

Elicit from students why increases and decreases in prices are often expressed as percentages. Work though the examples with the class and then set the tasks.

Answers:
a. 150 divided by 100 gives 1.5 and multiplying 1.5 by 30 gives 45.
The new quantity is 150 kg minus 45 kg = 105 kg.
b. 64 divided by 100 gives 0.64 and multiplying 0.64 by 25 gives 16.
The new quantity is 64 cm plus 16 cm = 80 cm.

4.2 Pairwork/Small group work

Explain to students that they are now going to apply their percentage increase and decrease skills to a problem. Ask students to work in pairs, first analysing the problem and then calculating the cost of the purchasing choices. Pairs then compare their answers with another pair's.

Answers:

high-street bookshop
25 divided by 100 gives 0.25 and multiplying 0.25 by 35 gives 8.75.
The sale price is £25 minus £8.75 = £16.25.

online bookstore
18 divided by 100 gives 0.18 and multiplying 0.18 by 5 gives 0.90.
The sale price is £18 minus 90p = £17.10.

Task 5 Types of decimal number

5.1 Individual work/Pairwork

If your students use English as an additional language, you may need to pre-teach the following vocabulary:
digit
number
finite number
Students may like to add this vocabulary to their list of statistics vocabulary. When presenting the three types of decimal number, elicit further examples from the class and then set the task.

Answers:
a. T – 3.678888888... is a recurring decimal number because some digits in the decimal part of the number are repeated endlessly.
b. F – 0.259876 is an exact decimal number because the decimal part of the number has a finite number of digits.
c. T – 4465.87555411025 is an exact decimal number because the decimal part of the number has a finite number of digits.

Task 6 Adding and subtracting decimal numbers

6.1 & 6.2 Individual work/Pairwork

Ask students to complete the task individually, and then compare their answers with a partner's.

Answers:
6.1

a.

	2	3	3	.	7	0
	0	8	9	.	0	0
+	0	0	1	.	5	5
	3	2	4	.	2	5

b.

	0	1	6	.	5	2	9
	4	2	7	.	6	0	0
+	0	0	5	.	9	3	0
	4	5	0	.	0	5	9

6.2

a.

	5	5	2	.	9	0	0
-	0	6	3	.	3	2	7
	4	8	9	.	5	7	3

b.

	0	0	9	.	5	0	0	0
-	0	0	2	.	8	7	5	4
	0	0	6	.	6	2	4	6

Reflect

These tasks could be set for homework.

Answers:
a. 90% of 30 = 27
20% of 75 = 15
5% of 60 = 3
50% of 44 = 22
So, in numerical order, starting with the smallest in the list and ending with the largest:
5% of 60   20% of 75   50% of 44   90% of 30
b. 970 – 45.38 = 924.62
65.298 + 1.2 + 397 = 463.498
55.7 – 3.441 = 52.259
So, in numerical order, starting with the smallest in the list and ending with the largest:
55.7 – 3.441   65.298 + 1.2 + 397   970 – 45.38

If you intend to teach *Unit 2* next, you may wish to ask students to bring to the next class a magazine or newspaper article that describes the results of an opinion poll in preparation for *Task 1.2*.

2 What is *statistics*?

At the end of this unit, students will be able to:
• understand the purpose of statistics
• recognise different types of variables

Task 1 What is *statistics*?

Ask students whether statistics play a part in their (future) disciplines, and if so, how they are used.

If your students use English as an additional language, you may need to teach the difference between statistics used as an uncountable noun, the subject of study, and statistics used as a plural noun, meaning numerical data. Students may like to add these terms to their lists of statistics vocabulary.

1.1 Pairwork

Ask students to work in pairs, matching stages to the examples given.

Answers:
a. 4
b. 2
c. 1
d. 3

1.2 Individual work/Small group work

If you have asked students to bring their own examples of opinion poll articles to class, they could work on this task individually. Alternatively, you could provide an article for students to work on in small groups.

Answers:
Answers will depend on the article chosen.

Task 2 Data for different subjects

2.1 Pairwork

Students follow instructions in the Student's Book.
Ask students to explain why and to whom the data might be of interest.

Answers:
Answers will vary from student to student, but may include:
a. healthcare
    1. The percentage of patients who arrive late for their appointment.
    2. The number of nurses working in a hospital.
    3. The most common injury that occurs in a workplace.
b. politics
    1. The percentage of politicians who are female.
    2. The number of residents who do not vote in a local election.
    3. The most popular reason for supporting a specific political party.
c. business
    1. The percentage of employees who have been promoted in the past year.
    2. The number of companies that employ more than 25 people.
    3. The most popular mode of transport for commuting to work.

Task 3 Variable types

If your students use English as an additional language, you may need to spend some time introducing the technical vocabulary of variables.

3.1 & 3.2 Pairwork

Ask students to work through the tasks together. Students may wish to add the technical vocabulary of this task, e.g., **qualitative data**, **quantitative data**; **continuous variable**, **discrete variable**, to their lists of statistics vocabulary.

Answers:
3.1
a. **Qualitative** because the colour of a dress in a clothes shop cannot be described using numbers.
b. **Qualitative** because the preferred hot drink of a person in a hotel cannot be described using numbers.
c. **Quantitative** because the number of biscuits in a packet can be counted or measured on a numerical scale.
d. **Quantitative** because the number of pencils in a box can be counted or measured on a numerical scale.

3.2
a. T – Weight of crisps in a bag is a continuous variable because it can take any value within a specific range.
b. F – Nationality of people visiting a museum is not a discrete variable because it is a qualitative variable and therefore cannot be classified as discrete or continuous.
c. F – Number of letters in a post-box is not a continuous variable because it can only take specific numbers.
d. T – Number of apples in a fruit bowl is a discrete variable because it can only take specific numbers.

3.3 Pairwork

Students work together to complete the table. In the feedback stage, elicit why quantitative variables are neither discrete nor continuous.

Answers:

variable	data	quantitative or qualitative?	discrete or continuous or neither?
breed	greyhound	qualitative	neither
length of tail	33 cm	quantitative	continuous
number of walks in a week	14	quantitative	discrete
colour	black	qualitative	neither
weight	32.5 kg	quantitative	continuous
number of toys owned	8	quantitative	discrete

3.4 Individual work

Some students will find this task easier to do if given a context to work within, e.g., further variables in relation to the friend's dog in *Task 3.3*.

Answers:
Answers will vary from student to student. However, taking the example of the friend's dog:
a. qualitative – favourite foods
b. quantitative and discrete – number of teeth
c. quantitative and continuous – height

If you set this as an open task, sample answers may include:
a. 1. Favourite holiday destination.
    2. Genre of films currently being screened at a cinema.
    1. Number of people in an exercise class at a sports centre.
    2. Number of purchases made by customers in a coffee shop.
    1. Length of screws manufactured in a factory.
    2. Height of players in a basketball team.

3 Collecting data

At the end of this unit, students will:
- understand why sample data is used
- learn how to write a questionnaire
- use interview questions to collect different types of data

Task 1 Populations and samples

Work through the introduction to *Task 1* with your students, eliciting the difference between a **population** and a **sample**. Students may like to add these terms to their list of statistics vocabulary.

1.1, 1.2 & 1.3 Pairwork

Students follow instructions in the Student's Book.

Answers:
1.1
a. No – It would be very time consuming to ask all the people living in London their favourite colour.
b. Yes – It would be fairly easy because all of the population works in one location.
c. No – It would be very expensive to make contact with such a large population.

1.2
Advantages of choosing a sample for data collection include:
- If the members of the population are geographically located in a wide area, it can be less expensive to contact a sample of people who are located in one area.
- If the population consists of a very large number of people, it can be less time consuming to ask questions of a smaller sample of people.

1.3
a. population = all the employees of the company worldwide
b. sample = the employees in the New York office

Students may point out that the New York office employees could be an unrepresentative sample, leading neatly on to the next task.

Task 2 Bias in sampling

Elicit examples of sentences using the term **bias** and write them on the board. Then ask them to read the introduction to *Task 2* and compare the meaning of bias given there with those of the sentences on the board.
Students may like to add the term a **biased sample** to their list of statistics vocabulary.

2.1 Pairwork

Set the task, emphasising the need for students to give reasons for their answers.

Answers:
a. The people leaving a supermarket with a trolley full of shopping are likely to prefer to do their shopping in a supermarket rather than to visit independent shops.
b. The teenagers purchasing tickets to see a horror film are likely to prefer seeing this genre of film at the cinema.

Task 3 Open and closed questions

This task also includes technical terms your students may like to add to their list of statistics vocabulary, e.g., **researcher**, **participant**; **open questions**, **closed questions**.

3.1 Pairwork

Ask students to read the introduction to the task and then work in pairs to complete the activity.

Answers:
a. Open – The participant can give any response they choose.
b. Closed – The participant must choose from the answers provided.
c. Closed – The participant must choose from the answers provided.
d. Open – The participant can give any response they choose.

3.2 Small group work

Pairs of pairs now discuss the benefits and problems of using open and closed questions in a questionnaire in terms of the researcher and the participants.

Answers:
a. For the researcher, open questions can provide interesting information about the topic under investigation, but the responses are difficult to analyse using statistical methods. Closed questions are easier to analyse, but they provide limited information about the opinions of the participant.
b. For the participant, open questions can be time consuming to answer, but they allow the participant to express their views more thoroughly. Closed questions are less time consuming to answer, but sometimes the participant feels restricted by the possible responses.

Task 4 Types of interview questions

4.1 Pairwork

Introduce the five types of interview questions and then ask students to complete the task in pairs.

Answers:

question	question group
Do you feel safe when you travel alone by train?	feelings
How many times did you travel overseas last year?	facts about past events
Do you agree or disagree with this statement? *Tourism causes problems because demand for holiday homes makes housing too expensive for local people.*	opinions
Which currency is used in Ecuador?	general knowledge
Do you own a car?	current facts

You could ask students to add a further example of a question on travel and tourism to each category.

4.2 Pairwork

Introduce the topic of protecting the rainforests. Ask your students to prepare five interview questions, one from each category. Then ask pairs of pairs to work together in small groups. Each pair reads aloud their questions, which the other pair categorises.

Possible answers:

question	question group
Do you feel sad when you hear that an animal is in danger of extinction?	feelings
How many times have you watched a television documentary about rainforests in the last month?	facts about past events
Do you agree or disagree with this statement? *The balance of the earth's eco-system will be disrupted if rainforests are destroyed.*	opinions
What is the name of the largest tropical rainforest?	general knowledge
Do you donate to a charity that aims to protect rainforests?	current facts

Reflect

Ask pairs to work on this in class, and write up their answers for homework.

Answers:
a. Interview – the researcher is able to have a conversation with the participant.
b. Online questionnaire – the participant answers the questions without the researcher being present.
c. Online questionnaire – the participant answers the questions without the researcher being present.

Universities require students to apply for ethical clearance for many types of research. Ask students to find ethical clearance information for their (future) university and to report back in a later class.

4 Organising data using tables and calculations

At the end of this unit, students will be able to:
• use a frequency table for displaying data
• interpret two-way tables
• calculate averages

Task 1 Making a frequency table

Ask students to read the two examples. Elicit the advantage of presenting data in a frequency table over presenting data in its raw state and what needs to be included in a frequency table. This task includes terms that your students may like to add to their list of statistics vocabulary, e.g., **frequency**, **frequency table**, **collected data values**.

1.1 Pairwork/Small group work

Ask students to work in pairs and then explain their method for accomplishing the task to another pair of students.

Answers:

number of breakfasts	frequency
0	1
1	8
2	7
3	7
4	5
5	1
6	4
7	7
total	40

1.2 Pairwork

Ask students to work in pairs constructing a frequency table, and then to draw a conclusion from the table.

Answers:

hot drink	frequency
tea	6
coffee	9
hot chocolate	5
total	20

1.3 Small group work

Students follow instructions in the Student's Book.

Answers:
a. F – Multiplying the values in the frequency column (= checkouts) by number of customers shows that there were 98 customers queuing at supermarket checkouts.
b. T – 16 checkouts had less than three customers in their queue (2 + 5 + 9 = 16).
c. F – Adding the frequency values for three, four and five customers shows that there were 21 checkouts with more than two customers queuing (12 + 6 + 3 = 21).

Task 2 Two-way tables

Discuss the example given in the introduction. Elicit what the two qualitative variables are (wears glasses and gender).

2.1 Individual work/Pairwork

Ask students to complete the sentences basing their answers on the table. They should then compare their answers with a partner's.

Answers:
a. In total, 237 children were asked about the way they usually travel to school.
b. The most popular way of travelling to school was walking.
c. More boys than girls took the bus to school.
d. More girls than boys gave a response to the question: 'How do you usually travel to school each morning?'

2.2 Pairwork

Ask students to read the information and elicit the two qualitative variables (homeowner and intention to vote). Then ask students to work in pairs, constructing a two-way table, using the *information given* to calculate **information not given**.

Answers:

		intention to vote			
		yes	no	undecided	**total**
homeowner	yes	*54*	*38*	**25**	*117*
	no	**9**	**18**	16	**43**
	total	*63*	**56**	**41**	*160*

Task 3 Finding the mode, median and mean

Read the introduction to *Task 3* with your students. Students may like to add **mode**, **median** and **mean** to their list of statistics vocabulary.

3.1 Pairwork

Students work on this task in pairs.

Answer:
This data set does not have a mode because there is no data value that occurs more often than the others.

3.2 Individual work/Pairwork

Students work on this task individually, and then compare their answers with a partner's.

Answers:
a. The sum of the data values is 80 and there are 16 values, so the mean is 80/16 = 5.
b. The sum of the data values is 352 and there are 11 values, so the mean is 352/11 = 32.

3.3 Individual work/Pairwork

Students work on this task individually, and then compare their answers with a partner's.

Answers:
c. 3 – The mid-way point between the two data values closest to the middle is 3.

Reflect

Ask students to work in pairs.

Answers:
a. F – The mean cannot be calculated for qualitative data because there are no numerical values.
b. T – If more than one data value occurs most often, then the set of data has more than one mode.
c. F – The median and the mean may be the same for a data set, but they could also be different.

5 Presenting data using graphs and charts

At the end of this unit, students will be able to:
*   identify when to use pie charts and bar charts
*   understand line graphs
*   draw scatter diagrams for quantitative data
*   avoid common mistakes with graphs and charts

Task 1 Pie charts

Read the introduction to *Task 1* with your students, eliciting the term for a proportion of the pie chart (segment).

1.1 Pairwork

Students read and discuss the statements in pairs.

Answers:
a. F – 25% of people said 'sometimes', and 25% of 200 respondents = 50 people.
b. T – The segment labels show that 15% of people responded with 'often' whereas only 10% said 'rarely'.
c. T – The segment labels show that 50% of people responded with 'never' and half that amount, 25%, said 'sometimes'.
d. F – The pie chart shows that 15% of the people said 'often', and 15% of 200 is 30 people.

1.2 Pairwork

If students find this task hard, ask them to reread the introduction to *Task 1*.

Answers:
The presentation could be improved by including a more meaningful title and segment labels so that the information presented is clear.

Task 2 Bar charts

Work through the introduction. If your students use English as an additional language, you may need to teach them the term **axis**, and its irregular plural **axes**.

2.1 Pairwork

Students follow instructions in the Student's Book.

Answers:
a.   200 girls – this can be calculated by adding the height (or length) of each bar.
b.   No – 20 girls preferred blue, while 50 girls preferred red as can be seen from the relative heights (or lengths) of the two bars.
c.   80 girls selected pink as their favourite colour as shown by the height (or length) of the bar representing pink.
d.   Black was least popular because it has the shortest bar in the chart.

2.2 Individual work

Students follow instructions in the Student's Book.

Answers:
a.

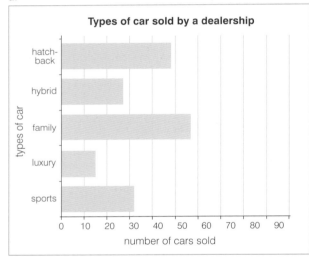

b.

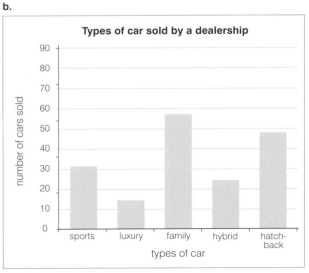

Task 3 Line graphs

Work through the example line graph in the introduction to the task, eliciting why a line graph would not be appropriate for displaying the car data in *Task 2.2*.

3.1 Pairwork

Ask students to discuss the data in pairs, looking for the main highlights, before writing the three sentences.

Answers:
Answers will vary from student to student, but may include:
• The line graph shows that there were more students enrolled on the course in year 5 compared to year 1.
• The largest increase in enrolled students occurred between years 4 and 5.
• The number of enrolled students decreased between years 2 and 3.

3.2 Pairwork

Students follow instructions in the Student's Book.

Answer:
The researcher would not be able to use a line graph to display the results because none of the data relate to change over time.

Task 4 Scatter diagrams

Work through the example scatter diagram in the introduction to *Task 4*, asking students why the data points are not joined with a line.

4.1 Small group work

Students follow instructions in the Student's Book.

Answer:
a.   As height increases weight increases.

4.2 Individual work/Pairwork

Students complete this task individually, and then compare their answers with a partner's.

Answer:

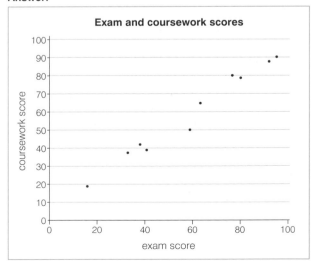

Task 5 Avoiding common mistakes

With Student's Book closed, ask students to predict some of the most common mistakes made when presenting data in graphs and chars. Then ask students to read the introduction to *Task 5*, checking whether their predictions are mentioned.

5.1 Small group work

Students compare the pairs of charts in terms of clarity of presentation of the data.

Answers:

a. The pie chart on the left side provides the best representation of the data set because the use of three-dimensional effects in the right-hand pie chart distorts the visual perception of the segment sizes, e.g., 'no' (17%) appears to be substantially larger than 'don't know' (29%).

b. The bar chart on the right side provides the best representation of the data set because the use of a background image in the left-hand bar chart distracts the reader's attention from the data presented.

Ask students to draw a conclusion from the task, e.g., clarity should drive the choice of presentation format.

5.2 Pairwork

The guidelines produced by students could form a wall display.

Possible answers:

*   Choose the graphical method that is most suitable to represent your results, depending on the type of data collected and the information you are trying to show.
*   Keep your diagram simple, avoiding three-dimensional effects and background images.
*   Ensure that both axes are clearly labelled with a useful title including units of measurement, if appropriate.
*   Use a short but meaningful title that describes the data displayed in the diagram.
*   When you have finished constructing your chart or drawing your graph, check that the meaning of the data and the results cannot be misinterpreted by the audience.

Reflect

Ask students to work in pairs.

Answers:

a. A line graph could be used to show the change in average tuition fee for an undergraduate course because the data is quantitative and changes over time.

b. A bar chart would be appropriate for showing the number of boxes of popcorn sold at a cinema on a Saturday evening because the data is qualitative and categorised.

c. A pie chart could be used to show the different lunch choices of employees in a company because the data is qualitative and we are interested in proportions.

6 Reporting your results

At the end of this unit, students will be able to:

*   make comparisons using graphs and charts
*   understand the importance of explaining terminology
*   summarise your results

Task 1 Comparing qualitative data

Discuss the example of a grouped bar chart given in the introduction to the task, eliciting how this bar chart is different from the one in *Task 5.1b* on page 26 of the Students Book.

1.1 Small group work

Students follow instructions in the Student's Book.

Answers:

a. T – The bar representing ham & pineapple pizza topping for girls is longer than for boys, so more girls prefer this pizza topping compared to boys.

b. F – Chicken feast is not the longest bar for the boys and so it is not the most popular pizza topping for them.

c. F – The shortest bar for boys represents cheese & tomato and so this is the least popular topping for boys; however, the bars for the preferences of girls show that hot & spicy is the least popular topping.

d. T – Comparing the two bars representing hot & spicy, we can see that more boys prefer hot and spicy pizza topping compared to girls because the boys' bar is longer than the girls'.

1.2 Small group work

Ask the groups of students to discuss the data, looking for four similarities and differences in preference between children and adults. Students should write up these sentences individually, and then the group should choose the best four sentences.

Answers:

Answers will vary, but may include:

a. The same number of adults and children preferred to read adventure books on holiday.

b. The least popular genre for both adults and children was history.

c. More adults prefer books about crime compared to children.

d. The most popular type of book for children was fantasy.

Task 2 Comparing quantitative data

Discuss the line graph in the introduction. Ask students what the legend on this graph says (city 1, city 2). If students are keeping a statistics vocabulary list, they should add the term **legend** to it.

2.1 Pairwork

Students follow instructions in the Student's Book.

Answers:
a. October – the lines intersect for this month.
b. No – for city 1, the wettest month was December, while for city 2, it was April.
c. September
d. November and December

2.2 Individual work/Small group work

Ask students to work individually drawing their graphs, and then compare their work with others' in a small group.

Students may note that the label for the axis showing temperature in the Student's Book should include the unit of measurement.

Answer:

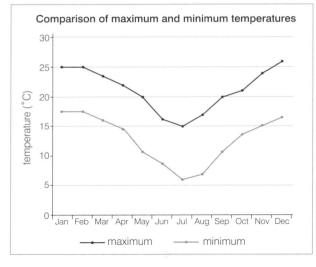

Task 3 Mathematical terminology

If students are keeping a list of statistics vocabulary, they could refer to it to help them with this task.

3.1 Individual work/Small group work

Students should write up the explanations individually, and then the group should choose the best four sentences.

Possible answers:
a. Variable: a characteristic or an attribute that can have different values; an example is the height of a person.
b. Sample: a subset of members selected from the population of interest.
c. Median: the middle value, which divides an ordered data set into two halves.
d. Line graph: a diagram used to display quantitative data collected at specific time intervals.

Note: Students' answers will contain their own examples.

Task 4 Summarising results

Discuss the example provided in *Task 4*, revising the difference between mode and median.

4.1 & 4.2 Individual work/Pairwork

Students discuss their ideas with a partner and then write a paragraph individually.

Possible answer:
Using the table values, we can see that a higher percentage of boys passed the mathematics test in comparison to girls. However, the mean score indicates that on average, girls scored more than boys and so we might conclude that the girls in this class perform better than the boys in general. The mode in this table does not tell us any information about the relative performance based on gender.

Reflect

This task could be set for homework.

Answers:
Answers will vary from student to student.